To Be a Priest

TO BE A PRIEST

Perspectives on Vocation and Ordination

---

edited by ROBERT E. TERWILLIGER
URBAN T. HOLMES, III

with a Foreword by John Maury Allin

1975

A Crossroad Book
THE SEABURY PRESS • NEW YORK

The Seabury Press
815 Second Avenue
New York, N.Y. 10017

LIBRARY OF CONGRESS CATALOGING IN PUBLICATION DATA

Main entry under title:

To be a priest.

  "A Crossroad book."
  Bibliography: p.
  1. Priests—Addresses, essays, lectures.
2. Priesthood—Addresses, essays, lectures. I. Terwilliger, Robert E. II. Holmes, Urban Tigner, 1930–
BV662.T6   262'.14   75–28248
ISBN 0–8164–2592–2

contents

foreword

By the end of the 1973 General Convention of the Episcopal Church in Louisville, I was convinced that the grave and potentially divisive issue of the ordination of women was one of those pastoral, theological and ecumenical problems which could not be resolved simply by voting. Some desired dramatic action immediately. Others seemed to be stalling for time, hoping the question would eventually go away.

I came to my new responsibility as Presiding Bishop convinced that the Church has the capacity as a community to resolve correctly and justly such problems when provided the opportunity and the means. Accordingly, I proposed to the House of Bishops that the Presiding Bishop-elect initiate a new process which would provide the membership of the Church, and any others interested, opportunity and means to share in this problem-solving. The bishops gave unanimous approval.

The purpose of the proposed process was to develop throughout the Church a clearer and more definitive understanding of the doctrine of Christian priesthood and a valid Christian concept of human sexuality. To secure a resolution of the ordination question in accord with the faith of the Church, a method was required to stimulate and enrich thoughtful discussions of priesthood and sexuality among church people.

The plan developed was to publish a book of brief essays on each subject. Representative and qualified authors were to be sought by co-editors who held differing views on the subjects. Each book was to include an extensive bibliography. I hoped each book would be a mosaic of written statements, each contributing to the form, depth, and color of the subject.

A committee was asked to check out the plan, suggest specific topics and titles and possible authors, and submit bibliographies. I asked John Goodbody and the Church Center Communication Staff to coordinate the process. The publishing services of the Seabury Press were available.

This book is the first mosaic. It is offered with the prayer that within it and from it some revealing light will be focused on priesthood. If from this book some questions receive answers, some answers receive clarifications, and some new questions are provoked, the purpose will be well served.

This book is not the official report of a "blue ribbon" committee. It is, rather, a sharing of understandings, a contribution to a process of community building, an attempt to clarify the meaning of priesthood and hopefully to reflect a clearer vision of Jesus, the Great High Priest.

I hope you will want to share this mosaic with others.

John Maury Allin
Presiding Bishop
The Episcopal Church

preface

At this moment in the history of the Church, attention is being focused intensely on the nature of the Christian ministry. This concern centers particularly on the ministerial priesthood and the episcopate. The immediate cause of this is, of course, the debate about the ordination of women. There has also been the long-continuing "crisis in ministry" with its anguished questions of identity and personal vocation. The Church has, in consequence, the mandate to explore in depth a theological issue which has much wider ramifications than the relationship of sexuality to ordination. This book is a response to that opportunity in essays which embrace a wide range of related topics.

In selecting subjects and essayists the two editors have sought to present a balance of viewpoint, drawing on various traditions and sources. There is, by intention, considerable disagreement among the authors, since we believe it is important for the readers to be exposed to many points of view to stimulate their thinking. In a volume such as this not every essay is directed to the same audience nor written on the same level. Our intention is that these contributions should reflect the best in current scholarship, yet at the same time be intelligible to both priest and layman.

We think it is important for the readers to understand that the two editors themselves have differing opinions on the matter of the ordination of women. At the same time we found a freedom to work together, which combined a natural collaboration with a kind of independence. Each of us does not necessarily sponsor every article in the book, but we have found it easy to live in peace with one another in the presence of this fact. This is, we think, a sign that it is possible to have a basic difference of opinion and still be in Christian fellowship within the same Church. We are both committed to a thorough theological appraisal of the nature of priesthood and its relationship to the Church, which we think is reflected in this book.

It should also be clear that in contributing to the volume no author is endorsing the opinions of his fellow essayists; each article stands by itself. Only the editors of the book have read all the articles, and the opinions of one person should not be attributed to anyone else who is part of this study.

In assembling the essays, we have sought to follow a general outline, which should become apparent to anyone working through the contents. We have begun with four essays with distinct points of view on the definition of priesthood. This is followed by a number of articles on biblical and historical themes related to the ministerial priesthood. After that is a section that deals with the functions priests perform, and we conclude with an examination of the priestly vocation today.

The reader should keep clear in his mind the difference between ministry and the priesthood. We do not understand these terms in any sense to be synonymous, and this volume is directed only toward the issue of priesthood and the related subject matter of the episcopate. We do not claim that the volume is in any sense exhaustive of the subject, although we do think it is representative. Undoubtedly some will criticize it for not having a particular point of view or group represented among the essayists. We have made a conscientious effort to draw on both men and women, Anglicans and non-Anglicans who have a particular interest in the subject of priesthood, people who are in favor of the ordination of women to the priesthood, and people who are not, and scholars throughout the United States and elsewhere. Undoubtedly, in a venture of this kind it is not possible to have everything in proportion; and sometimes the inability—for good reasons—of some persons to comply with our request for an essay has upset that balance a bit more. However, we do think that this volume embodies a fair representation of opinion in the Episcopal Church and beyond.

We do hope that the readers of this book will not be Episcopalians only. The essays represent substantial work, and although they do not in every instance contain new scholarship, they do make available a valuable summary of considerable research in the field on the part of distinguished theologians, historians, biblical and liturgical scholars.

In conclusion, we would note that while these are times of deep division on some very basic issues in the life of the Church, they are not times of darkness. The belief of the two editors is that in such times light often breaks through the rifts in the unity of the Church of Christ, and we have great hope that a deeper understanding of the ministry, and particularly of the priesthood, in the life of the Church will be the result of the struggle in which we are presently engaged. This book is offered as a contribution to that understanding.

Robert E. Terwilliger
Urban T. Holmes

PART I

What is a Priest?

chapter 1

WHAT IS A PRIEST?
One Anglican View

Robert E. Terwilliger

God has given us a priest—this is the Gospel. There are other ways of stating the Gospel, but this is an essential way because it is an essential way of seeing Jesus Christ: "We have a great high priest."

Jesus Christ is the one and only priest. This is the teaching of the New Testament. The most powerful expression of the unique priesthood of Christ is the Epistle to the Hebrews. He is the "high priest of our confession" (Hebrews 3:1). He is "not a high priest who is unable to sympathize with our weaknesses, but one who in every respect was tempted as we are, yet without sinning" (Hebrews 4:15). He is made priest by God himself who declares both "Thou art my Son, today have I begotten thee" and, also, "Thou art a priest for ever after the order of Melchizedeck" (Hebrews 5:5–6).

The writer fastens on this mysterious figure of Melchizedeck from the Old Testament. He appears in Genesis as the priest-king of Salem, "king of righteousness," "king of peace." Melchizedeck is the vivid symbol of the strange uniqueness of the priesthood of Christ because he appears "without father or mother or genealogy, and has neither beginning of days nor end of life, but resembling the Son of God he continues a priest for ever" (Hebrews 7:3).

Jesus is the end of all other priesthoods. He is not just a priest among priests; he is not another one in the line of priests, or a member of a caste of priests. The priesthood of Christ is the termination, but also the fulfillment of the priesthood of the Old Covenant. That is the significance of all this strange business about Melchizedeck. His priesthood is absolutely new, and comes from God's own act establishing the New Covenant through Christ's self-sacrifice: "He has no need, like those high priests, to offer sacrifices daily, first for his own sins and then for

3

those of the people; he did this once for all when he offered up himself" (Hebrews 7:27). This redeeming act uniting God and man forever gives Christians confidence to enter into the very presence of God now and in eternity.

The priesthood of Christ comes from the obedience of Christ. This talk about priesthood is not just cultic pious language, the stuff of mystic vision. It is grounded in the moral decisions of Christ which throughout his life led him to his death. It is grounded in his compelling awareness that he was called to be "the saving person," the one who must become the destroyer of those powers which separate man from God—sin, pain, and death—and be the sacrifice for sin, pouring out his life even unto its end.

The priesthood of Christ is determined by the concrete choices of a particular man, Jesus, who was driven by love to undertake a specific, dangerous risk, a course that led him to his execution. There is nothing romantic about it; it is as earthy and real as his sweating in the Garden of Gethsemane and his crying out in desperation on the cross. But there is God in it too: God, acting in all this, participating in all this, in his own strange shocking way of liberating man from guilt and evil, bringing him back to himself. "God was in Christ reconciling the world to himself" (II Corinthians 5:19).

The living, the dying, and the rising of Christ make him our priest; that is, they unite mankind to God in him. He is our mediator. This is the witness of the whole New Testament. It is left to the Epistle to the Hebrews to articulate this explicitly, but all four Gospels and every other book in the New Testament states the theme in different ways. Jesus is not just teacher, example, or "Christ figure." He is the Redeemer, the deliverer who does something for humanity which humanity cannot do for itself.

Mankind needs a priest; our race is separated from God. The biblical idea of sin, which permeates our self-understanding when it is truly Christian, sees man as self-centered, self-serving, self-destructive, alienated from God, and contaminated in his presence. Many people are afraid of this radical realism in the Christian doctrine of man. They can only bear to speak about man as created in the image of God, and to think of our way to God as simply a matter of our own initiative and our innate good impulses. Classic Christian belief has always insisted that we have to have someone between, a mediator uniting God to man in himself because he did something powerful and sacrificial. That powerful and sacrificial thing, the cross and resurrection, both seen together as one act of God, reveal him to be the priest of the Cosmos, the Word, the Logos, the Conquering Light who lightens every man, so that "the new and living way" back to God through Jesus Christ our Lord is at the heart of the universe and pertains to all men who come into the world, whether they know his name or not.

In times of relative prosperity and peace, Christians become self-satisfied about human nature and dangerously optimistic about man. There are signs that this naïve unrealism is now going away in the presence of an uncertain future. It is easy to lose the sense of our need for deliverance, and even to come to think of salvation as nothing more than therapy. One consequence of this is to regard priesthood in purely human and functional terms. The priest is understood to be just a person who is chosen by a religious community to represent the community to God and God to the community. He is recognized, perhaps because of his gifts and competence, and set apart by some official act to do this professionally. In his person he gathers the community symbolically to himself as the offerer of prayer and sacrifice to God, and he speaks and acts on behalf of God toward them all. There is no such concept in the New Testament. To put it bluntly: this concept belongs to a different religion.

There is only one priest, Jesus Christ. He and he alone can bond God and man because of what he did for us, and because of what he is as the incarnate unity of God and man. This essential Christian perception is movingly expressed in the eucharistic hymn of William Bright:

> Look, Father, look, on his anointed face,
> And only look on us as found in him.

The priesthood of Christ is sent forth into the world. The commission of the apostles is part of the Gospel. Jesus projects what he is and what he does for man into history in the persons of other men. He chooses, definitely chooses and designates, the Twelve to go forth in his name. They are to be not merely teachers and examples but extensions of himself and his divine mission. "He who receives you receives me, and he who receives me receives him who sent me" (Matthew 10:40). The full power of this sending was manifest after the Resurrection, when the apostles acted so explicitly in the name of Christ.

Perhaps this can be best seen in Paul, particularly in the authority of Paul made clear in his letters to the churches. He acts not as a vicar of Christ, one who is there in the absence of Christ, but as one through whom Christ himself is acting.

It is through the ministry of apostles that the Church is brought into being and built up. They do act as ministers of the Church and in the Church, but they are, above all, apostles *to* the Church. They represent the continual coming of Christ to the Church and the world.

In the New Testament the Church is spoken of as a priestly community. The language of priesthood is actually used of Christ and of the Church, but not of the ministry. "The priesthood of all believers" is a phrase popularized during the Reformation, based on this New Testament precedent; however, it cannot mean the priesthood of each and every believer separately, but the priesthood of the whole body which is the body of Christ the priest, in whom all Christians are members together. The togetherness of the priestly body is the priesthood of Christ present in this world. The apostolate is the organ through which the priesthood of the Church together is created, focused, and actualized.

The commission given to the apostles was too much for them. They were sent to evangelize the world. Before long it became obvious that they had to fulfill their commission through others—apostolic men. The exact configuration of the ministry in the New Testament period, and the subapostolic period (the period after the apostles), is not possible to determine with the certainty we would like. It appears that the forms of ministry which developed were various but not chaotic. Out of the experience of the Church, and under the authority of the apostles and the apostolic teaching, there emerged a canon of ministry, just as there emerged a canon of Holy Scripture. This shortly took the final form of the Christian episcopate with assisting ministries of presbyters and deacons. In the second century both this shape of the ministry, and its significance as a continuation of the apostolic ministry, was accepted.

It is essential for the theology of the ministry to understand the inner meaning of this process. Just as the creation of the canon of the New Testament, by the choice of some among many primitive writings, as Holy Scripture was the work of the Holy Spirit, so we may also see the emergence of the episcopal form of apostolic ministry as the work of the Holy Spirit. Contemporaneous with this development came the formulation of the creeds of the Church. Scriptures, creeds, and ministry became the protection of the Church and the definition of its identity during the tumultuous days of early heresy and schism. They are, all three, best understood as works of the Spirit which came through the works of men.

The Christian bishop came to be recognized as the essential high priestly presence, through whom the high priesthood of Christ functioned in the Church. He was the presiding figure at the Eucharist, not standing at the table to represent the local Christian community but uniting their Eucharist to all other Eucharists, because he is bishop in the whole Church and a form of Christ's participation in the Church.

When in the third century presbyters were commissioned to celebrate, this concept of priesthood persisted in their ministry. They represented not just the local congregation but the apostolic universality of the high priesthood of Christ creating the Church eucharistic. This they possessed by virtue of the laying on of hands by the bishop. The priest was seen as the minister of Christ *to* his Church to be the agency and the guarantor of the Eucharist to assure the sacramental presence of the body and blood of the risen Christ.

No man takes the apostolic ministry upon himself. This absolutely essential principle was realized by the Church in its early Spirit-formed years. This is the principle of ordination. The laying on of hands by the bishop represents the commission of Christ in his Church; and further-more, it is the means whereby the man ordained is united with the priesthood of Christ. No man has any priesthood of his own; it is only by the power of the Holy Spirit that the one priesthood of Christ can be shared out among his shepherds. This has nothing to do with man's goodness, his grace, his gifts. It has also nothing to do with his insuffi-ciency or sin. A man is made a priest, be he bishop or presbyter, only by the bestowal of the Spirit. Thus the Church continued and continues to actualize the commission of the risen Christ to his apostles:

> Receive the Holy Spirit.
> If you forgive the sins of
> any, they are forgiven; if
> you retain the sins of any,
> they are retained (John 20:22).

Ordination is a gift of the Holy Spirit. In these days of new awareness of the Spirit it is urgent for Christians to repossess their sense of the work of the Spirit in the whole life of the body of Christ. The Church is that community which exists by the continual invocation of the Holy Spirit. Its life is not its own. It has its existence and its identity only because of the perpetual coming of the Spirit.

The charismatic movement has made us freshly cognizant of the charisms, the gifts of the Holy Spirit, which are bestowed on the mem-bers of the Church in variety and power. We have learned again that there are many ministries, many services, within the Church which the Spirit gives: tongues, teaching, prophecy, administration, and a myriad of others. And we have come to sense that the ministries, the services, are not rights, certainly not professional achievements, but gifts, pre-cisely *gifts*, given by the Spirit.

Ordination is also a charism, a sacramental charism. It is given as the Church invokes the Holy Spirit—Come Holy Ghost—and the bishop, laying on his hands, says in one form of words or another: "Receive the Holy Spirit."

Ordination to the sacramental priesthood is a giving of the Spirit to *make* a man a bishop or a presbyter; it is not a mere act of recognition of the gifts a man already possesses. It does not signify that this man is acknowledged by the community—certified, as it were—to be the sort of man who should be its spiritual leader, its minister of worship. The priest must do something no individual can do in his own strength: he must be the one through whom the living priesthood of Christ becomes active toward and within the Church. This can happen only by an act of God, the Holy Spirit of God.

Let no one say: Magic! If it be magic, it is the magic of the resurrected Lord and the day of Pentecost, of the Acts of the Apostles and the faith of the Church for centuries. It is rather an incarnational action in which, by the power of the Holy Spirit, Christ is born to us again in ministry. Yes, through an external as well as an internal movement in the world, in body as well as in spirit—but that is the way of the Spirit, for the Holy Spirit is not very spiritual.

Furthermore, this gift of the Spirit creates a new ontological reality, a new form of being for a man—he *is* a bishop; he *is* a priest. There is an "is-ness" about it. Western Catholic theology has had a way of speaking of ordination as a bestowal of "grace." This term is not untrue but it is insufficient. It is rather the gift of the life, power, and presence of God, of God the Holy Spirit. This does not mean that the ordained are saints. It means that God's power has been delivered into their hands and for their use of it they shall be held accountable. It is like all of God's gifts: there is a reckoning. As in the parable of the talents, there is an eschatological moment of truth.

Richard Church, Dean of St. Paul's in London, preached an ordination sermon about a century ago entitled "The Gift of the Spirit." I have been moved to paraphrase his words in my own charges at the ordination of bishops and priests. He speaks of ordination in this tremendous way:

The awful gift of his consecrating presence, to be prized and cherished and faithfully served, or to be despised and rejected—but never to be recalled. On whom the Holy Ghost has set his seal, the seal must remain either for blessing or for judgment. *Pascal and Other Sermons,* p. 119

Christian priesthood is apostolic priesthood. Its projection into history comes from the act of Christ choosing the Twelve, and goes on in the ways which the Church, obeying his example, continues the commission. It is a "ministry of presence," but it is far more than that. It is not just a ministry of being there, of being here and being there silent and inarticulate; it is a ministry of the Word, for he who is the great high priest is also the word made flesh.

Apostolic priesthood is a proclaiming priesthood. In the Anglican tradition when it is true to itself, the ministry of the sacraments is never separated from the ministry of the word. In the Fourth Gospel the passages about the bread of life, about breaking the bread which is Christ, can be understood equally as referring to the Eucharist or the word. This perception is also realized in the renewal of the liturgy when the celebration of the word of God is given equal place with the celebration of the sacrament. This balance must be present in the ministry. There should never be a bishop or a priest who cannot tell what he is or what he is doing. The "mass priest," or the purely "sacramental priest," is not a Christian concept of priesthood. But more positively, there must be a revitalization of the awareness that the priest is by ordination a man sent to be an evangelist, even in his sacramental acts. It is as unnatural as it is unrubrical not to have a sermon at a Eucharist —even if it is only one sentence long. Our catholicism must be an evangelical catholicism, and our priesthood an apostolic priesthood. For this to happen, the perception of the transcendent dimension of the ministry of the word will have to come again. There is more to the ministry of the word than preaching, but preaching is its central form. To renew preaching, it is as necessary to know what it is as to know how to do it.

Preaching is not just ministerial talking in a church, in a certain place at a certain time. A sermon is not an essay read from a pulpit. Preaching is the proclamation of the word of God by a servant of God. It is a meeting between God and his people with the preacher in between. To be a preacher is an awesome thing, just as to be a consecrator of bread and wine is an awesome thing. The preacher is the mediator of the word, he is a man engaged in an act of God, and responsible before both God and the people for what he says. The Church must recover the sense of the presence in preaching, and when this comes—and come it will—it will be seen again as a most natural priestly act.

It is particularly tragic that the vision of the bishop, the high priest, as preacher has almost left the Church. In ancient times his episcopal seat was thought of as a teacher's seat—a professorial chair, if you will —not a princely throne. Everything a bishop says is still listened to, even newsworthy, but the bishop's ministry of the word has been downgraded in the presence of the exaltation of the lesser ministry of administration. The power, the priestly power, of the bishop in the Church and in society can be exercised by his ministry of the word; above all, his must be an apostolic priesthood.

Beyond the actual service of preaching, the priest is in other ways the servant of the word. In the celebration of the sacraments he must proclaim their meaning by his acts and attitude—and in his face—far more than before. He is a man whose faith is exposed by his person. Not only must he face the congregation, but he must often lead reluctant and resisting people into new ways and deeper appreciation of the sacraments as much by his manner as by his teaching. If he acts as though he does not know what he is doing, does not like what he is doing, or does not believe in what he is doing, that word is plain and powerful. If, however, he is absorbed and awed by being an agent of God and the Church in the celebration of divine mysteries, it will not be lost. This is a way in which the word is expressed in holy deed with convincing power.

The priest is the presence of the word in the world. He is to be a man available at all times and in all places, not only to help but also to bring the Gospel. To be recognizable as a priest is not an act of pride, but of availability.

How often I have wished (wickedly) that I had not been available on airplanes or on the street, particularly in the streets of a great city, by those who know they have a right to me! How many times also I have found that the urgent question about life or death, sin or God, has come to me from someone who knew me for a priest, but did not know *me!* Because I was a priest, unknown, uninvolved in the past or future of such a person, I was called upon to speak some word. We do not know the times or the reasons why Christ comes in such a need. But if we cannot be found when we are needed . . . ?

A priest is a voice. His words are to be a sacramental vehicle of the Word of God in season and out of season. A Christian priest is a man to whom the Holy Spirit is given by ordination so that the priesthood of Christ can be actively present in him and through him, that by his ministry men may be reconciled to God. He is the living presence of the word that "God has given us a priest."

chapter 2

WHAT IS A PRIEST?
Another Anglican View

C. FitzSimons Allison

My fixed Principle is: that a Christianity without a Church exercising spiritual authority is vanity and dissolution.
Samuel Taylor Coleridge

The first step in understanding the nature of any Christian ministry is to recognize the overwhelming agreement in virtually every tradition in the history of the Church that a vocation to ministry must be twofold: it must be an inner call to the individual and it must be validated by the corporate body, the "holy folk." Neither one, without the other, is sufficient.

The second step is to appreciate the function and purpose of such ministry. The purpose of the duly authorized regularizing, authenticating, or validating of such ministry is to insure that the ministry be truly the ministry, that it perform the function and purpose of its existence. The priest is one form of this ministry and shares with all other forms its final authenticity as the purpose of ministry is fulfilled. This purpose is well expressed by St. Paul in Romans 15:16 in the phrase "the priestly service of the gospel of God . . ." It is the contention of this paper that priesthood derives its authenticity from its "service of the gospel."

Our present dilemma, in relation to the confusion concerning ministry and its eroding authority, is to see four ways in which ministry has been separated from its true purpose.

PRIESTHOOD NOT *SACERDOS*

"Priest" is the English word for "presbyter" (elder), and the latter is the only legitimate connotation for "priest." As the Roman Catholic *Encyclopedia of Theology* correctly points out: "It is important to bear in mind, in the following discussion of the applicability of the terms 'priest' and 'priesthood' to the office holders in the church, that the New Testament does not use the terms *hiereus, hierateuma,* to describe ecclesiastical office. They occur, however, in the interpretation of Christ's work of salvation and in the description of the New Testament people of God" (p. 1281). The Gospel's connection with priesthood is that after Christ's "one sacrifice once offered," priesthood in the *sacerdos* and *hiereus* function of offering sacrifice has been completely and finally done away with. As Bishop Lightfoot explains the Epistle to the Hebrews: "Now this apostolic writer teaches that all sacrifices had been consummated in the one Sacrifice, all priesthoods absorbed in the one Priest. The offering had been made once for all; and, as there were no more victims, there could be no more priests."[1]

Hence, Richard Hooker, theologian of the sixteenth century, preferred the term "presbyter" to "priest"[2] because he knew that the word "priest" in English, besides properly translating "presbyter," is also the only English word to translate *sacerdos* or *hiereus*, thus making way for the unwitting denial of the Gospel by slipping from the first to the second meaning of "priest."

Scripture does use the concept *hiereus*/priest, not for the ministry but for the whole Church, the holy folk. "But you are a chosen race, a royal priesthood, a holy nation, God's own people . . ." (I Peter 2:9). The Reformation doctrine of the "priesthood of all believers" gets its root from this text (and from the Epistle to the Hebrews) and has been greatly misunderstood in modern times, as if it were merely some democratic egalitarianism. For Luther and the Anglican reformers the doctrine meant not so much the priesthood of each believer but of all believers. All baptized persons share equally in this priesthood as members of this "holy nation, this royal priesthood," this body, of which Christ is the head. However, it did not mean the "presbyterate of all believers." For both Luther[3] and Anglicanism, the presbyter must be lawfully called and sent by duly constituted authorities before he exercises this ministry (cf. article XXIII).

This brings us to the question of how this presbyter/priest is related to that sacrifice of Christ. There are three ways this connection is made. The presbyter/priest does not make the sacrifice as the old *sacerdos*/priest did but he now *represents* that event as elder of the folk, the Church, this whole "royal priesthood," this whole Christian ministry. As he represents the Church his ministry relates all to Christ's completed sacrifice and its benefits. He is not a mediator between God and his people, but he is a representative person of this holy folk, the people of God, the body of Christ. Secondly, this priesthood relates us to that once-for-all sacrifice of Christ by the preaching of the word, the Good News. As in the text from Paul (Romans 15:16), "The priestly service of the gospel of God" is the function and purpose of this ministry. It is extremely important to note that whereas *hiereus* is never used to describe the Christian ministry in the New Testament, it is here used to describe the function of the Gospel. It is the Gospel that mediates and relates us to Christ. The ministry does so as it is a servant of this Word. Thirdly, as the presbyter presides at the holy table the once-for-all sacrifice is presented in word and action, and this body, the Church, is united anew with its head (Christ) in his sacrifice. As the report of the archbishop's commission, *Doctrine in the Church of England,* so well puts it: "But if the Eucharist is thus spoken of as a sacrifice, it must be understood as a sacrifice in which (to speak as exactly as the subject allows) we do not offer Christ but in which Christ unites us with Himself in the self-offering of the life that was 'obedient unto death, yea the death of the Cross.' "[4]

Hence the true meaning of priest is lost by its association with the Old Testament priesthood which has been done away with by Christ. The meaning of priest is recovered by the presbyter/priesthood fulfilling its purpose as servant of this Gospel.

TOO NARROW DOCTRINE OF VALIDITY

The second way in which ministry has been separated from its purpose is by a too narrow and simplistic doctrine of *validity.* However necessary some guidelines must be, the adequacy of the traditional requirements for validity—the proper intention, form, and matter—is increasingly questioned on all sides. John Jay Hughes, the Roman Catholic protagonist for recognition of Anglican orders, cites some very important difficulties increasingly shared by us all concerning such criteria for judging validity of ordination:

One example of these problems is that the existing concept of apostolic succession leads to recognizing the validity of the orders possessed by eccentric *episcopi vagantes,* clerical rolling stones who display considerably greater interest in ritual, ceremonial and a valid "succession" than in belief, and whose numerically tiny churches, despite their grandiose titles, possess more clergy than laity. How can one be happy with standards of validity which treat the Archbishop of Canterbury as a layman while recognizing as valid, or possibly valid, the "orders" of prelates claiming to be Bishops, Archbishops, Apostolic Pontiffs, Patriarchs, Exarchs, Ruling Prelates or Sacred Beatitudes in such bodies as the Autonomous African Universal Church, the Orthodox Keltic Church of the British Commonwealth of Nations, the Old Catholic Church (Integrated Rite), the Old Catholic Evangelical Church of God, the Apostolic Church of St. Peter, the Ancient Catholic Church, the Universal Apostolic Church of Life, the Pre-Nicene Catholic Church and the Old Roman Catholic Church, Caer-Glow

Province of Great Britain—most of these august organizations possessing only a single place of worship, consisting more often than not of a back room somewhere in the dreary wastes of outer London?[5]

To recall one of the purposes of ministry, the safeguarding of the Gospel and doctrine, is to raise serious questions as to the effectiveness of such concepts of validity. Is anyone really comfortable with a doctrine of validity that might depend upon the thread of *one* (three are required for regularity, *one* for validity) bishop in apostolic succession. In 1939, Bishop Hensley Henson wrote: "The Church of England, at the present time, exhibits a doctrinal incoherence which has no parallel in any other church claiming to be traditionally orthodox." If that was true in 1939, little has occurred since then to reassure us that our Anglican polity has been an altogether effective guardian of the apostolic faith.

Hence priesthood loses its vitality and integrity when it attempts to define "validity" in isolation from its function and purpose of serving the Gospel.

PREOCCUPATION WITH CREDENTIALS

The third way in which the purpose of ministry has been frustrated is the tendency to be preoccupied with credentials alone. John Henry Newman, in 1833, set the tone of this preoccupation with his first tract, "Hard Master He would not be to bid us oppose the world and not give us the *credentials* for doing so" (italics mine). For over a century a strong tradition in Anglicanism has presented the credentials of a ministry in apostolic succession (quite narrowly defined) as the *esse* of the Church; that is, to be without it is not to be the Church. Hence, in spite of the refusal of Reformation Anglicans or the official Anglican formularies to specify dogmatically what particular form of ministry or polity is essential, this tradition of Anglicans did not hesitate to unchurch "non-conformists" who shared their commitment to Scripture, creeds, and ecumenical councils, and who for centuries had manifested at least as much "fruit" as had we in the Anglican communion.

Opposed to this exclusive position were those who, following Richard Hooker, refused to elevate a particular polity to the level of dogmatic essence. Hooker's argument with the Puritans was precisely along the lines that no one can be sure what, if any, particular form of polity is prescribed by Scripture. The most we could claim was that our threefold polity of bishops, priests, and deacons was historical, primitive, and not un-Scriptural. Hooker's restraint has held up far better than the dogmatic claims of his contemporary antagonists or his successors' exclusive position in the light of modern scholarship.

The Anglican Articles of Religion and the Preface to the Ordinal omit any claim that our polity is enjoined in Scripture, or that it is the only valid form of Christian ministry, or even that it is the best form. Anglicans are simply required to recognize that it is a valid form and not contrary to Scripture. Article 36 affirms that the Anglican ordinal contains nothing "superstitious and ungodly," nor is it to be regarded as a defective form of ordaining the ministry.

The exclusive position largely begun with the tractarians in the nineteenth century, came to be called the *esse* view (that valid orders, not just for the Church of England but for all Christians everywhere, required ordination by bishops in apostolic succession, without which there could be no valid sacraments nor any true Church) and was opposed by the *bene esse* view (that such ordination was for the "well-being" of the Church). One's head or liver, for instance, is of the *esse* of being human, whereas one's ear or arm is of the *bene esse*.

The *esse* position was claimed for a long time, not only as a position within the Anglican Church but the only true position, and that it was the view historically held by the Anglican Communion. Historical studies have for some time proven this latter claim untenable. Even the Anglo-Catholic leader, Dr. Darwell Stone, acknowledged this:

But I think that we have now to face the facts that, so far as the Reformation and post-Reformation formularies and divines are concerned, there are loopholes which we can use but not the support for an exclusive position."[6]

There have been frantic attempts, however, to maintain this exclusive position in spite of the overwhelming contrary evidence, especially that produced by Norman Sykes in *Old Priest and New Presbyter*. The most judicious view of this whole controversy is perhaps that of the Anglo-Catholic bishop, A. E. J. Rawlinson:

... despite the attempts so insistently made in post-Tractarian times by Anglo-Catholic Theologians to stiffen up the Anglican claim for Episcopacy and to treat it as being of the actual *esse* of the Church, the attitude of the classical theologians of Anglicanism in the age of the Carolines did not involve quite this assertion. The conclusions reached by the Dean in *Old Priest and New Presbyter* are not in fact likely to be upset. The defenders of Anglicanism in the 16th and early 17th centuries, however emphatic their claims for Episcopacy, nevertheless did not, with one or two possible exceptions, go so far as to "unchurch" foreign Protestant Churches. The change of opinion on the question of Episcopacy which came about in the 19th century was due to the influence of the Tractarians and of their successors the Anglo-Catholics. The "exclusive" theory of Episcopacy (to use the late Dr. Darwell Stone's epithet) is today widely prevalent among the clergy of the Church, though it is less widespread among the laity. Its upholders are more vocal than those of the "Evangelical" school; it may be doubted whether they are more numerous. They are a "school of thought" within Anglicanism, and their view is permissible; but it is very unlikely to be adopted as the official doctrine of the Church.[7]

The contrast between the clergy and laity mentioned by Bishop Rawlinson should not be overlooked. The sociological factors that would naturally lead more clergy than lay persons to increasing emphasis upon credentials are hard to exaggerate. A poll in England in 1973 showed 87.7 percent of the Anglican clergy in favor of eventual union with Roman Catholics versus 57.85 percent of the laity for that outcome. On the other hand, only 27.7 percent of the clergy were for eventual union with Congregationalists, versus 72.2 percent of the laity who were for reunion in this direction.[8] One can hardly explain this discrepancy on the basis of doctrine and theology.

The widespread relinquishing of the *esse* position (cf. K. M. Carey, ed. *The Historic Episcopate*, Dacre Press, 2nd ed. 1960) is not so much due to taking account of the historical scholarship that was long ignored by otherwise responsible scholars (e.g., Kenneth Kirk, *The Apostolic Ministry*, 1957 edition with preface by A. M. Farrer, Hodder and Stoughton, London), but to the fact that this *esse* position no longer served to safeguard what Anglo-Catholics so highly—and often correctly—valued. Especially in the case of the reunion of the Churches in South India and in discussions with American Methodists, it became apparent that episcopacy and the *esse* position could no longer be counted on to assure true "catholicity," whatever one's definition of that may be.

Hence, the events of history itself have forced us to return from the exclusive preoccupation with credentials to associate ministry again with its doctrinal and Gospel purpose.

DENIGRATION OF DOCTRINE

The fourth way the ministry has been separated from its purpose is the increasing disinclination of the Church to deal with doctrine. No sensitive person can be unsympathetic with Church officials for their reluctance to open up what is, if not a Pandora's box, certainly an explosive and perhaps divisive enterprise. When the demand for some official response to Bishop James Pike's doctrine resulted in the publication of the book *Theological Freedom and Social Responsibility* (ed. S. F. Bayne, The Seabury Press, 1967), the recommendation was that, "the word 'heresy' should be abandoned except in the context of the radical, creative theological controversies in the early formative years of Christian doctrine" (p. 22). Although there were some wise and helpful things said in the report and the associated papers, it could hardly be claimed that this was a bold and confident willingness to maintain and proclaim the doctrine and teaching of classical Christianity.

William Temple faced a similar issue earlier in this century in regard to the problem of treating the touchy and possibly centrifugal issue of doctrine in the ecumenical movement. He insisted that it could not forever be ignored or delayed. He was opposed on all sides by those who maintained that "service unites; doctrine divides" and that he would tear apart this tenuous association by bringing into it questions of "faith and order." We are all the beneficiaries of his courage and wisdom in helping to bring about the great World Councils on Faith and Order.

If the Church could take the real risk in following Temple's example, it would face and understand afresh the theological and doctrinal issues without which our understanding of priesthood will be continuously impoverished. From the time of Scripture, Ignatius, and Iranaeus, the ministry has been seen as the expression and guardian of unity and doctrine. Of the eight vows publicly acknowledged by the candidate in the Prayer Book service of the ordination of a priest, four of them are explicitly concerned with the responsibility for maintaining *doctrine*. Hence the authority of priesthood is derived from its engagement in its function and purpose, preserving and manifesting the unity and doctrine of the Christian faith.

"What He did not assume, He could not redeem."—Athanasius. One of the values in associating again the ministry with Christian doctrine is the light thereby shown on the nature of priesthood. Athanasius' insight concerning Christ, insists that the soteriological (e.g., the salvation of man) purpose of the Incarnation is paramount; it was truly, completely, and fully man that the Logos assumed in the Incarnation. This dictum became the hallmark of orthodox Christianity against the prevailing atmosphere so uncongenial to the New Testament's portrait of a fully human Jesus.

That Jesus was a male must not, then, mean the exclusion of women from salvation. Jesus' humanity must include all humanity lest they be not saved. It would seem, therefore, that his maleness in the work of salvation is *personal* and not *sexual*. Theologians agree that all masculine pronouns, when used of God, are to be understood to mean not *sexual* but *personal*. God is not a *male* but he is our *personal* God, not an *it*. Just such considerations as these should guide us in considering who may represent the Church as priest/presbyter. It would seem that for the Church to exclude a woman believing herself truly called to priesthood merely on the grounds of sex would be confusing what is essentially *personal* with what is merely *sexual*, what is a matter of *humanity* with what is a matter of *gender*.

PRIEST / PARSON

There is a long history of confusion regarding what name to call a priest. As we have seen, the New Testament understanding of priest-hood has no Old Testament *sacerdos/hiereus* function, but this order is set aside to serve the Gospel and represent the whole body. There is great power in a name, and we must be quite careful by what names we are called. Not to have some name that distinguishes the priest from the laity is to overlook the special functions and distinctions between clergy and laity that have existed from the time of "the 70" through and including virtually all traditions of Christendom. But to name a name that distinguishes *and* separates is to violate the common priesthood/ *hiereus* character of members of this "holy nation," this "royal priest-hood."

The term "Mister" does not seem to satisfy the need to express the special representative character of priest, and the term "Father" would tend to deny the priesthood participated in by all baptized people. It needs to be added that it is difficult to understand how "Father" can be used without seeming to encourage hierarchical temptations of the clergy and at the same time nurturing infantilism in the laity. This latter is a particularly acute and often justifiable criticism by psychologists of the results of conventional distortions of Christianity. The issue is whether God works through Christ, then the ministry, to the Church; or through Christ, then the Church, through which he calls and sends his ministry. The latter is clearly a more "catholic" as well as more biblical view. It is not the ministry which makes the Church but the Church which makes the ministry.

Over the centuries the Church in England evoked from the faithful a name for the priest: parson. It was sometimes used pejoratively and is now regarded as quaint. But it was the English word for "person," the "person" of the parish, of the congregation. The sacramental nature of the office *worked*. The faithful being called on knew their "parson" had come, the congregation was represented to them in this person. I remember quite vividly a few years ago lying in a hospital recovering from surgery. Coleman McGehee, the rector of my parish church came to see me. I was glad to see him as a delightful and affectionate friend but even more as my "parson," the person representing those people of God who had helped set him apart and paid him a salary to represent them, to be their "person." The name seems to carry as none other the New Testament function of priest, the priest/presbyter, who in his person shows the true priesthood of all believers, by whom God is known in this world, and who is set apart to maintain Christian doctrine and unity by "the priestly service of the gospel."

NOTES

1. J. B. Lightfoot, *The Christian Ministry* (New York: T. Whittaker, 1883), p. 141.

2. Richard Hooker, *Of the Laws of Ecclesiastical Polity*, vol. 2, (New York: E. P. Dutton & Co., Inc., 1954) pp. 429, 432.

3. "... no one may make use of this power except by consent of the community or the call of the superior." G. Rupp, *The Righteousness of God* (Naperville, Ill.: Alec R. Allenson, Inc., 1953), pp. 315–316.

4. *Doctrine in the Church of England* (London: S.P.C.K., 1938), p. 162.

5. John Jay Hughes, *Stewards of the Lord: A Reappraisal of Anglican Orders* (New York: Sheed and Ward, 1970), pp. 2, 3.

6. Quoted in Norman Sykes, *Old Priest and New Presbyter* (London & New York: Cambridge University Press, 1956), p. 211.

7. *The Anglican Communion in Christendom* (London: S.P.C.K., 1960), pp. 57–58 and 49–52.

8. Reported in *The Living Church*, 22 (July 1973).

chapter 3

WHAT IS A PRIEST?
An Orthodox Statement

Thomas Hopko

The following remarks are intended as a brief *apologia* for what I understand to be the theological and spiritual vision of the sacrament of the priesthood in the Christian Church. I believe that this vision is rooted in the Church's understanding of God as the Holy Trinity, with salvation experienced as communion with God the Father through his incarnate Son Jesus Christ by the Holy Spirit in the Church, which is Christ's body and bride.

The Christian faith in its orthodox, catholic expression, has always confessed that the Godhead is a Trinity of persons in perfect unity and community. The one true and living God is God the Father. He is the creator of heaven and earth, the Lord of Israel, and the Father of Jesus Christ. The one true and living God is not, and even cannot be, alone in his divinity. His divine perfection is such that from all eternity he has with himself, by his very nature, his personal, divine, and uncreated Son who is his personal Logos, his image; and his Holy Spirit who is the personal realization of his divine activity and life. There is by nature and not by will, by essence and not by decision, a divine Trinity of persons who are one, consubstantial, and undivided divinity: the Father and the Son and the Holy Spirit.

According to the same orthodox, catholic faith, humanity is created in the image and according to the likeness of divinity. Human nature is the created expression of the uncreated nature of God the Father, the Son, and the Holy Spirit. The multipersonal character of human being and life is the created expression of the fact that humanity cannot be in God's image and likeness unless there are many persons who bear the exact same nature in a community of being which is reflective of the uncreated Trinity.

Also it must be defended, even if it has not been specifically ex-plicated in the past, that the male and female nature of humanity is essential to its being made in the image and likeness of God. Adam alone cannot be the image and glory of God. There must also be Eve if the human is to reflect the divine as its created expression and epi-phany. The tradition of faith is clear about the fact that Adam, the male, reflects God the Father by being made in the image of God's only begotten Son, his exact image and likeness as the divine person, who is incarnate of the Holy Spirit and the Virgin Mary, as the man Jesus. Eve exists necessarily and essentially with Adam as reflective on the level of creation of the Most Holy Spirit who proceeds from the Father and rests in the Son. As the Holy Spirit is the divine person of the Trinity who is the Spirit of God and the Spirit of God's Son, and as God himself and his Son could not exist without the Holy Spirit, so Adam could not exist as the created image of God and his Son without Eve, together with whom he shares and communicates in the being and life of the Most Holy Trinity.

God the Father does not exist without his Son and his Spirit. There is no Son without the Spirit, and no Spirit without the Son. And so, in the order of creation, there is no Adam without Eve, and no Eve with-out Adam. And as the Son is not the Spirit, and the Spirit is not the Son; so also Adam is not Eve, and Eve is not Adam. And as the Son is not of another nature than the Spirit and is not superior to the Spirit as a person, so also Adam is not of another nature than Eve and is not superior to Eve as a person. For as divinity is a community of essentially equal persons; so humanity, made in the image of God, is a community of essentially equal persons expressing the life of its divine prototype, the interpersonal life whose content is love.

Within this same theological vision, Adam is understood as the high priest of creation. His essential vocation, as made in the image of God's uncreated Son, is to offer all things to the Father by the grace and power of the Spirit. Essential to Adam's vocation as high priest is the existence of Eve. Adam is not merely "incomplete" without Eve; he cannot even exist without her fulfilling his priesthood. There is no fulfillment of Adam as a person, reflecting the personhood of God's Son, if there is no person of Eve. It is Adam with Eve in perfect communion, the commu-nion of being and life in love, whose very existence is a priestly offering to the Father in adoration, thanksgiving, and praise. But Adam himself is the "type of the one who was to come" (Romans 5:14). The first Adam is the prefiguration of the final Adam in whom he finds fulfillment and according to whom, as the divine image of the invisible Father, he finds the source of his being. The "man of dust" is made to have life in the "man from heaven," the second and last Adam, the incarnate Son of

God, Jesus Christ, the only high priest of the Christian confession, made a priest forever according to the order of Melchizedek (Cf. Hebrews 3:1ff). Jesus Christ offers himself to the eternal Father through the eternal Spirit together with his new Eve which is God's good creation, deified in and with him by his very own Spirit as his body and his bride. This new creation and new humanity in Christ is now the Church, the new Eve, imaged in the symbol of the temple, the body, and the bride, and personified in the person of the Virgin Mother of Immanuel, Mary the Theotokos, who is filled with God's Spirit to be the new mother of the living, made divine by grace.

Jesus of Nazareth is the one great high priest who offers the one perfect sacrifice to God, which is himself and all of creation; or rather, which is all of creation embodied in himself as his deified body and divinized bride. Christ alone is the one and only priest. He is the one who, as St. John Chrysostom's liturgy puts it, "offers and is offered, receives and is given." He is the priest and he is the offering. He is the Logos and he is the lamb. He is the teacher and pastor, the healer and reconciler, the king and judge. He is the teacher and pastor because he is the disciple and the sheep. He is the healer and reconciler because he is the wounded and the forsaken. He is the king and judge because he is the slave and the condemned. He is *all;* and his being as all is the very essence of his priesthood as the last and final Adam who, in offering himself, offers all to his Father, who is the source of all.

The unique priesthood of Christ remains in the Church forever, because Christ himself remains forever in the Church. Christ is not absent from his Church. He is present. His body is not headless. His bride is not widowed. Christ is eternally present in the Church until the end of the ages. As present, he needs no vicar, no representative, no delegate. He needs no substitute to take his place, no *alter christus*. For he himself is here.

The sacrament of the priesthood in the Church, the ordained ministry, is, according to the catholic tradition, the sacrament of Christ's presence in the Church. It is the *mysterion* of the presence of the head and bridegroom with his body and his bride in all the fullness of his messianic presence and power, with all the fullness of grace and truth of the eternal life of the kingdom of God which he brings. Jesus Christ is present in the Church as its head and husband, king and lord, priest and pastor, prophet and teacher, reconciler and healer. The realization and manifestation of his presence is the sacrament of the ordained clergy which is an essential element of the one "great mystery ... Christ and the Church" (Ephesians 5:32).

There are those who deny this doctrine of the catholic tradition of the Church and this view of the ordained ministry. Some say that the

Church is an institution established by God with sacraments, defined as visible signs of invisible grace, instituted by Christ, one of which is the sacrament of the priesthood understood as the vicarious, delegated continuation and representation of the power and authority of Christ in the Church exercised by those individuals possessing this gift. Others say that the Church is indeed an institution established by God with sacraments so defined, but that the ordained ministry is not a sacrament because Christ is invisibly present in the Church which is itself essentially invisible, having human expressions within the life of this world which are necessarily limited, partial, and sinful. With the Church thus understood, the grace of God is given through faith with baptism and the Lord's supper generally understood, one way or another, as the only visible sacramental signs of this invisible grace working through faith. In this general view, the ordained ministry is essentially a ministry of preaching and administration, one of the many ministries of the Church, with Christ's unique priesthood operating within the community through the "priesthood of all believers." Thus, in a word, there is no sacramental sign and presence of Christ in the Church, and the clergy of the Church are functionaries of the body, possessing the professional qualifications for this service.

Both of these views, according to the orthodox faith, are wrong. They are wrong because they are expressions of a wrong understanding of the Church and a wrong understanding of the sacraments. The Church, to put it simplistically, and perhaps to risk a grave misunderstanding, is not an institution with sacraments understood as particular channels of grace existing within it. The Church is rather itself a sacrament, indeed *the* sacrament par excellence. It is the great mystery of new life in the new humanity of the new Adam in the new creation. It is, as it were, the new Eve, the new mother of the living. It is a sacramental reality with sacramental expressions as its essential realization within the time and space of the old creation. It is itself the new creation and the new life in Christ, *one* with the unity of God; *holy* with his sanctity; *catholic* with his divine fullness; *apostolic* with his eternal mission of salvation through communion with himself. It is Christ's deified body by grace. It is Christ's glorious bride by love. It has purely human, historical institutions and organizations, but it is not essentially identified with them or defined by them. Its essential being is the mystery hidden for ages in God but now revealed to men, the mystery of man's salvation and deification in communion with God through the Son of God in the Holy Spirit. As such, it is the "church which is his body, the fulness of him who fills all in all" (Ephesians 1:23). It is the "church of the living God, the pillar and bulwark of the truth" (1 Timothy 3:15).

The ordained priesthood in the Church and for the Church—not without or apart from or over the Church—is the sacramental presence of Christ himself in and for the Church. It is the sacrament of Christ's abiding presence in the Church as its husband and head, priest and pastor, prophet and teacher, master and lord, forgiver, reconciler, healer. It is the mystery within the great mystery of Christ and the Church which guarantees the objective presence of salvation in the body, for it guarantees the objective presence of the Savior in all the fullness and power of his theandric, messianic activity. It is the sacrament which guarantees the objective identity and continuity of the Church in space and time—the so-called apostolic succession—because it manifests and realizes in the body the identity and continuity of the saving presence and activity in and for the Church of the "one mediator between God and men, the man Christ Jesus" (1 Timothy 2:5; cf. Hebrews 8–10).

The ordained priesthood in the Church exists to manifest and realize the priesthood of Christ, and so the priesthood of all Christian believers, in and for the body. For the priesthood of Christ and the priesthood of the believers are not two priesthoods; they are one and the same. The ordained, sacramental priesthood is the objective sacramental realization and expression within the Church of this one priesthood. The question whether the ordained priest, bishop or presbyter, represents Christ or represents the people is unanswerable. In the first place the ordained priest does not *represent* anyone. He *presents* Christ in the community and actualizes his presence in a sacramental way within the body. The Christ whose presence is manifested sacramentally in the Church is "the one mediator between God and men" whose unique, perfect, divine, and eternal priesthood—the only priesthood that exists —abides in the Church as its own priesthood in him as his body and his bride: ". . . a chosen race, a royal priesthood, a holy nation, God's own people" (1 Peter 2:9).

The priesthood of the head is the priesthood of the body. The priesthood of the husband becomes the priesthood of the bride. The priesthood of the Savior is the very priesthood of the saved. As Christ himself is the presentation (and not the representative) of God to man; so also is he the presentation of man to God. But he is the latter only because he is first the former. He takes us to the Father as his children only because he first brings his Father to us who were not his children, but the children of darkness and of the "father of lies." In like manner, the ordained priest in the Church presents the community to God because first and primarily he presents God in the community. "Where the bishop appears, *there* let the people be, just as where Jesus Christ is, *there* is the catholic Church" (St. Ignatius of Antioch, *To the Smyrneans* 8:2).

This is the doctrine of the catholic Church from the beginning, and not only from the beginning of the history of the new covenant Church, but from the beginning of creation itself. For the initiative is always God's. His action is always "first." And we might even dare to say that this is so not only "from the beginning" but even "in the beginning" when from the Uncreated Arche of the Father, the eternal Son of God, is timelessly generated, together with the eternal procession of God's Holy Spirit, the only begotten Son of God for whom and by whom all things are made to be his body and his bride by the indwelling of his Spirit in the communion of divine life, whose essence is love. This is the testimony of the Scriptures, the prophets, the apostles, and the saints. This is the witness of the sacramental life of the Church and its canonical tradition. We find this testimony in Hosea, Jeremiah, and Isaiah. We find it in Saint Paul. We find it in Ignatius of Antioch, Gregory of Nyssa, John Chrysostom, and John of the Cross. We find it symbolized in the sacramental rites of baptism, the Eucharist, marriage, and ordination. We find it in the canons which insure the proper churchly life. Yahweh is the husband of Israel. Christ is the husband of the Church. The husband and wife reflect the great mystery of Christ and the Church. And the ordained priest is married to his flock as the sacramental expression of Christ whose Church, filled by his Spirit, is his body and his bride.

The ordained priesthood is a sacrament of the Church. As such it is not an individual vocation or a personal charism. It is not one of the several ministries of the members of the Church. It is rather the sacramental ministry of the ministry of Christ, in whom all partial and personal ministries are fulfilled and by whom they are judged. In this sense it may be said that the ordained priest in the Church, as Jesus Christ himself, has no particular ministry and no individual vocation. He has none because he is the *term of reference* and *norm of evaluation* of all. And so, in the opposite way, it may be said that the ordained priest has all vocations, precisely because, by the very sacramental nature of his being a priest in the Church of Christ, he has none in particular.

The sacramental priest exists in and for the Church, being himself a human member of the Church, as the living *term of reference* for all personal and individual vocations and ministries of the members of the Church. He is the one whose sacramental vocation it is to be the sign and the presence, and in a sense even the judge, of the value and significance of all human activities and modes of existence. He is the pastor who witnesses to the pastoral dimension of all human vocations. He is the priest who testifies that all human being and life must be offered to God in Christ by the grace of the Spirit. He is the teacher whose presence is the measure and norm for all human teaching. He is the judge whose very presence judges all who execute justice. He is the healer who demonstrates what healing is. He is the servant reminding all who serve of the purpose of their ministry. He is, in a word, the sign of the presence of Christ and the expression of his presence in the Church as the source and the goal, the content and the judge, of all human life and activity.

With such a sacramental vocation, the qualifications for being a priest in Christ's Church are not reducible to any purely human talents or skills. The priest must teach, but he need not be a theologian. He must preach, but rhetorical eloquence is not a necessity. He must shepherd the flock, but he need not be a specialist in pastoral counseling. He must administer, but purely executive gifts may belong to another. Of course he must pray, but the particular charism of prayer is not a requirement. The qualifications which a priest must necessarily possess are traditionally external rather than internal. His specific charisms may vary, but his objective image must be vivid and firm. He must be a male member of the Church, physically whole, totally identified with the faith of the Church and professing it soundly and clearly. He must be of spotless reputation to those inside and outside the Church. He must have no record of grave sin after baptism, specifically including the shedding of blood, sexual immorality, or public deceit. He must be the husband of one wife or a celibate virgin. If he is married, the wife and children within his household must be members of the Church with similar qualifications. He must not be involved in political, economic, or military affairs or in any secular business; nor can his wife. His individual talents and gifts must be such that they do not conflict with his sacramental being and life.

Thus, for example, should he feel called to a life of social activity, government service, monastic contemplation, or legal advocacy; or should he feel compelled to take a second wife, to join the military, to pursue an academic career, or to propagate one or another specific form of Christian activity or piety, he must give up his sacramental office. In a word, the ordained priest is a sacramental image, an animate symbol, a living sign and expression of Christ in whom dwells bodily all the fullness of God. He is not necessarily the bearer of specific gifts, the most gifts, or the best gifts. He is not the holiest member of the Church. He is not the one who takes the faith most seriously. He certainly is not the one who has a "religious vocation." Every human being has a "religious vocation" simply because every human being is made in the image and likeness of God, as an Adam or as an Eve. And there is no doubt that most human beings are more talented and more skilled in one or another specific way than is the priest. Certainly many members of the Church are personally more holy, including repentant sinners, handicapped persons, people twice married, and those who bear the humanity of Eve.

But this is beside the point. There is not some sort of "competition" between the bishops and presbyters in the Church and the rest of the members on the basis of talents, gifts, or personal sanctity. For the priesthood is not a profession, a job, or a way of self-fulfillment in personal holiness. It is a sacrament of the Church, in and for the Church, of him who is the Church's only pastor and priest, its head and its husband, the Lord Jesus Christ. Of course all will agree that the bearer of this sacrament should be holy and talented. But the holiness and the gifts are included within the sacrament, and the sacrament is not dependent on the sanctity and skills of its bearer. For this reason no person can claim the office of priesthood on the basis of professional qualifications or personal holiness. The priest is called by God with the consent of the faithful in ways known to himself. Some may force their way into the office for one reason or other, but this is a violation of the sacrament undertaken unto condemnation and judgment. For the priest is called and chosen by God as the sacramental guarantee of the continuity and identity, the purity and integrity, of the body and bride of his Son until he comes again in glory to establish his kingdom in which there will be no sacraments, for then he will be all and in all.

chapter 4

WHAT IS A PRIEST?
A Roman Catholic Catechism

Quentin Quesnell

PRELIMINARY

How can an individual theologian presume to speak for the Church today?

If it is possible for a person to be a Roman Catholic today, it is possible to state theologically what one means by being a Roman Catholic. A sound statement today would include the same elements as a sound theological statement at any time in the past. That means stating one's understanding of what Catholic teaching is, telling the sources from which one draws this understanding, and submitting one's work to possible correction by other theologians, to possible approval or disapproval by Church authorities, and to eventual acceptance or rejection by the community of fellow believers.

What are the sources for a theological position on the priesthood?

Scripture and Catholic tradition. Under Catholic tradition, first come all teachings recognized as defined dogmas; second, the teachings of councils, popes, the Synod of Bishops, official liturgical texts and practice; third, common beliefs, practices, and attitudes of the faithful as well as published sociological, psychological, and historical data on these; fourth, the writings of Catholic theologians based on other sources, with due allowance for reciprocity of influence.

What are the specific sources for this catechism?

a. The Second Vatican Council, especially the Dogmatic Constitution on the Church, *(Lumen Gentium);* and the decrees on the pastoral office of bishops *(Christus Dominus)* on sacerdotal training *(Optatam Totius),* and on the ministry and life of presbyters *(Presbyterorum Ordinis).*

29

b. The report of the 1971 Synod of Bishops on the ministerial priest-hood *(De Sacerdotio Ministeriali).*

c. The "Declaration in Defense of the Catholic Doctrine on the Church Against Certain Errors of the Present Day," issued by the Sacred Congregation for the Doctrine of the Faith on June 24, 1973, as ratified and confirmed by Paul VI.

d. Special attention has been given also to the doctrinal statements in the series of instructions with which the Pope has introduced the reformed rites of the Eucharist and other sacraments.

1. What is priesthood?

Priesthood is the state or office of persons recognized as able to mediate between human and divine beings, especially by the offering of sacrifice.

2. What is the Christian priesthood?

The Christian priesthood is the state or office of persons recognized as able to bring themselves and others closer to God by their offering of the one perfect sacrifice of Christ.

3. What is the one perfect sacrifice of Christ?

It is Christ's giving himself over to achieve the union of mankind with God our Father in perfect obedience and perfect love. Christ did this by accepting and fulfilling God's plan for salvation: that he should die on the cross and be raised from the dead that all might believe, and believing find life through his name.

4. How do those who share Christian priesthood bring themselves and others closer to God by offering the one perfect sacrifice of Christ?

In three ways: in love, in word, in liturgy.

a. In love, insofar as they believe the Gospel: that Christ gave himself for them, and that through his sacrifice God makes reconciliation to himself and one to another available to all. Believing this, they find themselves committed to Christ's love, so that as he gave himself for them, they would love and give themselves for one another.

b. In word, insofar as they offer to others the good news of salvation in Christ. As all persons come to appreciate what God has done for them in Christ, the world is transformed in the power of Christ's sacrifice.

c. In liturgy, insofar as they express their joy and thanks to God for his gift in Christ, especially when they do this together as a community, publicly marking important moments of life with the sign of Christ's sacrifice.

5. Who are the persons recognized as able to do these things in the Roman Catholic Church?

a. All who have received the sacrament of baptism are in the *state* of being able to do all these things.

b. All Christians who have received the sacrament of confirmation are in a *state* of personal mission and responsibility to do them, according to the measure of charismatic gifts each one receives from the Spirit. This implies not only a higher fidelity to Christian sacrificial love and liturgy, but in particular a special concern and readiness for spreading the word of the Gospel.

c. All confirmed Christians who have received the sacrament of holy orders have the office and the public responsibility to foster, promote, and facilitate the doing of them, according to the needs of the Church and according to the measure and kind of hierarchical gifts each one receives from the Spirit. Obviously this also implies greater personal fidelity to the sacrificial life of love, word, and liturgy. But it consists in accepting a public responsibility for the ministry of love, word, and liturgy.

6. Is priesthood through confirmation and through orders merely a higher degree of the priesthood to which one is consecrated in baptism?

Each of these three sacraments is a share in the one priesthood of Christ because each is a special consecration to uniting self and others to God through the sacrifice of Christ. Confirmation may be considered the completion of the baptismal priestly consecration, inasmuch as the charismatic gifts of the Spirit enable the confirmed to fulfill some aspect or other of the general mission which baptism implied.

But orders confers a specific responsibility toward the community as a whole—a responsibility which one would otherwise not have. The community has a right to demand the word of God and the sacraments from one who has been ordained. Thus, by orders one is committed not just to a higher degree or state of Christian living, but to a distinct kind of service.

7. Is the priesthood of baptism, confirmation, and orders permanent?

Not all who receive these sacraments always live in a manner worthy of their priestly consecration, cooperating with God's graces. Again, for some, external circumstances may block the exercise of their priesthood; such as interdict, excommunication, suspension. Finally, God's entire plan for any individual life can never be certainly predicted.

Nevertheless, the consecrations themselves remain a fact, known to the persons themselves and publicly recognized by the Church. They are, of their nature, as permanent as the needs of the Church they are supposed to serve and as the priesthood of Christ in which they are a share. They never need repeating.

8. What do you call the priesthood which results from orders?
The ministerial priesthood or the hierarchical priesthood.

9. Why is this priesthood called ministerial?
Because it consists in personally assuming a public responsibility for the ministries of love, word, and liturgy through which the Church shares in the sacrifice of Christ, uniting the world to God through him.

10. Why is this priesthood called hierarchical?
a. Because it commits the ordained to exercising, through their ministry, a "holy leadership" *(hierē archē)* in promoting the Church's sacrificial life.
b. Because this commitment is distributed hierarchically; i.e., according to a scale of ranks and orders.

11. What are the ranks and orders of the hierarchical priesthood in the Church today?
Three: bishops, presbyters, deacons.

12. What responsibilities are given to bishops?
The Church regards bishops as "priests of the first order," standing in the top rank of the hierarchical priesthood and possessing the fullness of the priesthood. Their responsibilites, then, are all those which Christ gives to his apostles in the four Gospels. Thus they accept primary active responsibility for promoting all the ministries of the Church—the many ways mankind can be brought closer to God by sharing in the sacrifice of Christ.

Bishops, therefore, oversee the ministry of the word (all officially Catholic teaching and preaching is done in union with bishops); the ministry of the liturgy (they preside, personally or through delegates, over all public services, programs, and rituals performed in the Church's name); and the ministry of charity (promoting and facilitating every kind of work of Christian love). This is a threefold office of teaching, ruling, and sanctifying.

13. What are presbyters in the Catholic Church today?
Presbyters are "priests of the second order." Their responsibility is public and personal, but secondary. They assume a share in the ministries for which the bishop has primary responsibility. The specification of which ministries and what share has varied according to differences

of time and place, the needs of the Church, and the decision of the bishops.

Presbyters are the persons whom Catholics commonly call priests; the persons whom Catholics encounter, for instance, in their parishes, performing the same general sort of functions which Christian clergymen perform in other Churches. The name "presbyter" is the precise term for them in the Latin official Church documents.

Over several hundred years of history "presbyter" evolved into the English word "priest" (cf. French *prêtre,* Italian *prete,* German *Priester*). But "presbyter" does not mean "priest," it means "elder." In a discussion like this one about the various kinds of priests in the Church, we cannot get along with just the word "priest." Presbyters are just one group among many who share Christ's priesthood, and one among the three who share the ministerial priesthood.

14. What are deacons?

Deacons are ordained persons belonging to the lowest rank of the hierarchy. They share in the ministries for which the bishop has primary responsibility.

15. Why are presbyters commonly called priests, while deacons are said to be ordained for service?

Among the ministries early and regularly assigned to presbyters was that of presiding over small local congregations in the bishop's name and in particular of presiding at the Eucharist. But the Eucharist is the public Church action most explicitly linked to the sacrifice and hence the priesthood of Christ. As the community's service of praise and thanks for God's gift in Christ, it has been from very early times understood as the Church's supreme act of sharing Christ's self-offering.

The one who leads the eucharistic service speaks Christ's words of offering and invitation: "This is my body, given for you. This is my blood, poured out for you." Since the presbyter was the one whom the people experienced regularly in this role, standing at the community's altar day after day, it was quite normal that they should come to speak of the presbyter as their priest par excellence.

The ministries confined to deacons in the early Church generally concerned more the material side of Church life: providing for the poor, the sick, widows and orphans; and administering Church property. In the course of time local presbyters took over these ministries too, and for all practical purposes the office of deacons simply disappeared for well over a thousand years. The diaconate was just a brief stage one passed through on one's way to the priesthood (presbyterate), and has been restored only since Vatican II.

16. Can you sum up these several uses of priesthood on a chart?

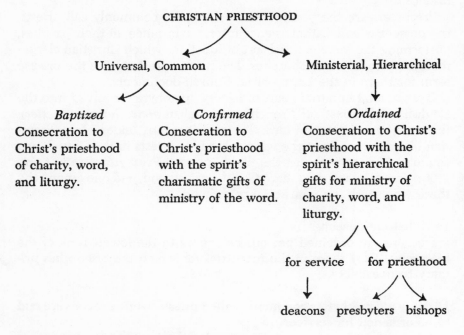

CHRISTIAN PRIESTHOOD

Universal, Common   Ministerial, Hierarchical

Baptized   *Confirmed*   *Ordained*
Consecration to   Consecration to   Consecration to Christ's
Christ's priesthood   Christ's priesthood   priesthood with the
of charity, word,   with the spirit's   spirit's hierarchical
and liturgy.   charismatic gifts of   gifts for ministry of
                        ministry of the word.   charity, word, and
                                                liturgy.

                                        for service   for priesthood

                                        deacons   presbyters   bishops

17. What is the sacrament of orders?

Orders is the sacrament in which persons able to act in the name of the Church publicly assign to mature fellow Christians publicly acknowledged responsibility for continuing in the Church the sacrifice of Christ through ministries of liturgy, words and love.

The *grace* symbolized *(res sacramenti)* is the sacrificial life of the Church in the power of Christ's cross and resurrection; including the special helps needed to minister to that life successfully.

The essential sign of that grace and the assurance that it will continue *(res et sacramentum)* is the public assigning and accepting of the responsibility. (This essential sign is, as in many other sacraments, itself symbolized by an external word and gesture [*sacramentum tantum et non res*]. At present, as often in the New Testament, this is the invocation of the Spirit and the laying on of hands (Cf. 1 Timothy 4:14; 2 Timothy 1:6; Acts 13:3).

Christ left the group of his disciples a mission to "make disciples of all nations, baptizing them . . . teaching them" (Matthew 28:19f.), and so gave the Church a lasting need for persons to assume the responsibilities that mission entails.

18. Why only "persons able to act in the name of the Church"?

Because all sacraments are administered by Christ through the Church.

19. Who are these persons?

They are the persons recognized as being able at the time and in the circumstances about which the question is posed. By a long-standing tradition and by present law, a bishop, together with some wider representation of the episcopate, ordains a bishop. A bishop, with the assistance if possible of some representation of the presbyterate, ordains a presbyter. A bishop or a properly delegated presbyter ordains a deacon.

20. Why say: "in order to assign a publicly acknowledged responsibility"?

As in all sacraments, the external action and words must be joined to a specific intention of doing what the Church wants done.

21. Why say: "to a mature Christian"?

To stress the fact that one should not ordain lightly. The person being ordained should have been baptized and confirmed, and should show some ability and readiness for the responsibilities in question.

22. Does "fellow Christian" mean Roman Catholic?

The one ordained must have been baptized. The one ordaining must be able to act in the name of the Church (as in #18, above). Since priesthood is permanent (#7, above), bishops continue to be recognized as able to ordain in the name of the Church even if they cease to be in union with Rome, so long as they maintain the intention of ordaining as the Church wants. Of its nature, all ordaining is for the life and health of the one Church, the one body of Christ.

23. Does "fellow Christian" mean male?

It includes male, but does not exclude female. By present canon law and a long tradition, women cannot validly receive this sacrament. But because of the considerable evidence that women were ordained deacons during several early centuries, theologians commonly hold today that the invalidity is strictly a matter of Church law, and that nothing in the nature of the sacrament prevents its being conferred on women. No official Church statement has contradicted this frequent and public teaching of respected theologians.

24. Does "fellow Christian" mean celibate?

No. In most rites of the Roman Catholic Church, most presbyters are married. In all rites, most deacons are married. Even the Latin (Western or Roman) rite does not declare the ordination of married persons invalid. But that one rite does require that those ordained promise to live in celibacy after ordination. Moreover, Church law declares any marriages contracted after ordination invalid without a dispensation from Rome.

25. Does this sacrament produce a real change in the person who receives it?

Catholic teaching is that every sacrament does what it signifies. In holy orders, the invocation of the Spirit with the laying on of hands signifies the public assigning and accepting of ministerial responsibilities for the sacrificial life of the Church. The public assigning and accepting of these signifies the continued life of the Church in the power of Christ's sacrifice. Since the sacrament does what it signifies, ordained persons actually do receive those responsibilities and actually do receive the hierarchical gifts of the Spirit to make them effective. Thus they are consecrated to a distinct priestly role (#6, above) and this consecration is permanent (#7, above).

26. But do they receive special powers?

Granting public responsibility to fulfill publicly recognized needs implies as well the powers necessary to fulfill the responsibility. Those given such charges—to "preach the word, be urgent in season and out of season, convince, rebuke, and exhort, . . . (2 Timothy 4:2); and to "Declare these things; exhort and reprove with all authority" (Titus 2:15)—obviously must have the power to do these things.

Those given the responsibility to listen to the penitents' confessions of sins and to speak words of forgiveness in the name of the Church, as Christ directed, must have the power to speak those words in the Church's name and with the full conviction that they are effective, as Christ said: "Whose sins you shall forgive, they are forgiven" (John 20:22). And so with the Eucharist and the other sacraments.

27. What if persons not ordained speak such words?

The report of the 1971 Synod of Bishops on the ministerial priesthood explains that "where the presence and action of the ordained ministry are missing, the Church cannot have full certainty of its fidelity and visible continuity" (Pars Prima, 4). Thus the sacramental ministration of persons not ordained, never publicly assigned or acknowledged for ministry in the Church at large (especially if these persons simply take the role upon themselves), is not recognized as valid by the Church. The 1973 "Declaration in Defense of the Catholic Doctrine on the Church Against Certain Errors of the Present Day" states this concretely in regard to the Eucharist.

This is not a matter of judging subjective intentions or dispositions, nor an attempt to shorten the arm of the Lord. Catholic theology has always held that "God is not limited to the sacraments." He gives grace and performs wonders where he wills. But the visible Church and the seven sacraments, like the Incarnation itself, are given to believers as assurances and security that here, at least, God may be found and found acting graciously. This assurance and security are found then at least in Christ, in his sacrifice, in the Church, and in the preaching and sacraments of the Church when done by persons publicly charged to do them in the Church's name.

The 1971 Synod of Bishops adds another reason. The ministry of those ordained by the Church "always tends to the unity of the whole Church and to calling all nations together within the Church" (Pars Prima, 6). But "every individual community of the faithful needs communion with a bishop and with the universal Church" (ibid.). Therefore, especially for its Eucharist, an individual community should have the presence of one ordained by the universal Church "in the service of unity" (ibid.).

28. Could a group of baptized persons, long and hopelessly isolated from other Christians, ordain a ministerial priesthood from among themselves?

Church law and teaching do not provide for all extraordinary circumstances. In such situations, people usually have to do the best they know how. If a group in desperation decides they should ordain, not in order to divide themselves from the rest of the Church but to help themselves remain as faithful as possible, the matter is for God to provide, not for theologians to judge (cf. #27, above). Should the isolated group ever again find contact with the rest of the Church, any remaining practical problems could be easily settled if they have maintained their desire to live in unity in the one body of Christ.

Most questions about truly extraordinary circumstances must receive similar answers; e.g., the seminary brain-teaser: What if some medieval prince-bishop, in malice or jest, once deliberately withheld his intention while supposedly ordaining another bishop? Would the sacramental ministrations of all bishops and priests dependent on that one simulated episcopal consecration be invalid down to the end of time?

29. What of subdeacons, of tonsure, and the four minor orders listed by the Council of Trent?

These have all been suppressed since Vatican II. They were required by Church law, not by the nature of the sacrament.

30. What of the teaching of the Council of Florence that the outward sign of the sacrament in ordaining a presbyter was "the handing over of the chalice with wine and the paten with bread" and the words: "receive the power of offering sacrifice . . ."?

Pope Pius XII declared: "If that was at one time necessary for validity, by the will and law of the Church, everyone knows that the Church can change or abrogate what it has legislated. . . . Therefore, We declare by our Apostolic Authority that if it ever was differently laid down in law, at least in the future the handing over of the instruments is not necessary for the validity of Orders" (Apostolic Constitution, *Sacramentum Ordinis*, 30 November 1947).

31. What of "laicized" priests?

This strange term comes from the distinction in Church law between the clerical state and the lay state. The clerical state is the collection of customs, rights, and duties with which law and tradition have surrounded ordained persons. It is the legally sanctioned clerical life-style, including the domicile, clothing, recreation, prayer, political action, etc., of ordained persons (cf. esp. Canons 124–144 in the *Codex Iuris Canonici*).

Since Vatican II, many presbyters have been dispensed from the Church law of celibacy (#24, above). Those dispensed are also removed from all the obligations and privileges of the clerical state and are assigned the obligations and privileges of the lay state (Canons 211–214). This has nothing to do with the reality of their ordination or the permanence of their ministerial priesthood (Canons 948–1011).

Confusion comes from the fact that the term "lay" is also used as the opposite of "priestly." In this sense of the word, the Council of Trent anathematized those who say "that a person who was once a priest can become a layman" (Session xxiii, 1563). The 1971 Synod of Bishops (Pars Prima, 5) and the 1973 declaration reaffirmed this as pertaining to the teaching of the faith. Thus the seven to ten thousand presbyters in the United States who have received dispensations from the law of celibacy are part of the ministerial priesthood along with the fifty-five thousand others who have not requested dispensations, even though the former belong to the lay state and the latter to the clerical state.

Adding to the confusion is the fact that current practice, summed up in a January 13, 1971, decree of the Sacred Congregation for the Doctrine of the Faith, is for bishops to inform dispensed priests they are forbidden any regular public exercise of the official ministry of the liturgy. This has led to the occasional popular use of such terms as "ex-priests," "former priests," etc.

The terminology in official Church documents was formerly "priests (presbyters) reduced to the lay state"; then "priests resigned from the active ministry." Most recently it is "dispensed priests" or simply "married priests."

32. What of Leo XIII's decision against the validity of Anglican orders?

Leo XIII decided according to the principles already discussed (esp. #17–20, above). His decision is commonly understood to have been practical; i.e., not a decision about historical or dogmatic fact but about the security with which Catholics could regard Anglican administration of the sacraments (cf. #27, above). The decision was based on the factual information available to him at the time, and has to be corrected by the better and fuller information about sixteenth-century English reforms which Roman Catholics generally have become aware of since his time.

33. Must the Catholic Church insist on the image of "priest"? Is it not a pagan leftover, redolent of abuses attacked by the prophets? Would not "pastor" or "minister" or "preacher" do as well?

All language uses images, all images bring dangers of misunderstanding. "Pastor" is the Latin word for shepherd. Ordained Christians should not treat people like sheep. "Minister" is Latin for "table-waiter." But that is not the clergy's only function. "Preacher" describes one task—but there are other things to be done.

Nor does the Bible clearly favor one image over others. Luke 22:26f uses the table-waiting image of Jesus and his disciples, but Acts restricts it to a group of seven who are distinguished by this from the apostles and their ministry "of prayer and service of the word" (Acts 6:2–4). (Cf. Matthew 23:11; Mark 10:43.)

In the Gospels, Jesus often uses "shepherd" of himself but never of the disciples. Ephesians 4:11 is the only New Testament text that uses it of Church workers. The corresponding verb, to shepherd and feed sheep, comes up only in the scene with Peter in the late addition to John's Gospel (21:15–17).

"Priest" brings the danger of confusion with the priesthood of the Old Testament, suggesting the multiplying of sacrifices, ritualism, influencing God, closeness to God reserved for the few, etc. Yet Hebrews 7–10 was given us to show that none of those should be found in Christianity; and yet that there is a deep value in using the imagery of priesthood and of sacrifice for Jesus' great act as well as for his Church's sharing that act through its life of love and service, its preaching, and its liturgical prayers, especially the Eucharist.

SOME NEW TESTAMENT TEXTS
ON THIS IMAGERY

Christ was "designated by God a high priest after the order of Melchizedek" (Hebrews 5:10). "When Christ came into the world, he said: 'Sacrifices and offerings thou hast not desired, but a body thou hast prepared for me; in burnt offerings and sin offerings thou hast taken no pleasure.' Then I said: 'Lo, I have come to do thy will, O God' " (Hebrews 10:5–7).

He came "to put away sin by the sacrifice of himself" (Hebrews 9:26). He "offered up himself" (Hebrews 7:27). He "loved us and gave himself up for us, a fragrant offering and sacrifice to God" (Ephesians 5:2). "He loved me and gave himself for me" (Galatians 2:20). He "is the expiation for our sins, and not for ours only but also for the sins of the whole world" (1 John 2:2).

We are called to share his sacrifice and his priesthood: He has "made us a kingdom, priests to his God and Father" (Revelation 1:5ff). "Come to him, to that living stone, rejected by men but in God's sight chosen and precious; and like living stones be yourselves built into a spiritual house, to be a holy priesthood, to offer spiritual sacrifices acceptable to God through Jesus Christ" (1 Peter 2:4ff).

"Do not neglect to do good and to share what you have, for such sacrifices are pleasing to God" (Hebrews 13:16). "Present your bodies as a living sacrifice, holy and acceptable to God, which is your spiritual worship" (Romans 12:1). "He laid down his life for us, and we ought to lay down our lives for the brethren"(1 John 3:16). A gift given in love becomes "a fragrant offering, a sacrifice acceptable and pleasing to God"(Philippians 4:18).

Paul is "a minister of Christ Jesus to the Gentiles in the priestly service of the gospel of God; so that the offering of the Gentiles may be acceptable" (Romans 15:16). He is "poured out as a libation upon the sacrificial offering of your faith"(Philippians 2:16f.). And "you are a royal priesthood, a holy nation, God's own people, that you may declare the wonderful deeds of him who called you out of darkness into his marvelous light"(1 Peter 2:9).

"Since we have confidence to enter the sanctuary by the blood of Jesus, . . . and since we have a great high priest over the house of God, let us draw near. . . . (Hebrews 10:19–22). "Through him let us continually offer up a sacrifice of praise to God, that is, the fruit of lips that acknowledge His name" (Heb 13:15).

"We have been sanctified through the offering of the body of Jesus Christ once for all"(Hebrews 10:10). "We have an altar from which those who serve the tent have no right to eat"(Hebrews 13:10). "The bread which we break, is it not a participation in the body of Christ? . . . Consider the practice of Israel; are not those who eat the sacrifices partners in the altar?"(1 Corinthians 10:16–18). "I received from the Lord what I also delivered to you, that the Lord Jesus on the night when he was betrayed took bread, and when he had given thanks, he broke it, and said: 'This is my body, which is for you. Do this in remembrance of me' "(1 Corinthians 11:23–25).

PART II

The Priesthood in the Bible and History

chapter 5

PRIESTHOOD IN THE HISTORY OF RELIGIONS

Joseph Kitagawa

According to Webster, the term "priest" is the contracted form of "presbyter" (Greek, *presbyteros,* "older" or "elder"; akin to Sanskrit, *purogava,* "leader," often referred to a leader of a herd of cattle). This term is used to describe, on the one hand, a general category of cultic practitioners who perform sacrificial, mediatorial, interpretive, and ministerial functions; and on the other, those who have clearly defined sacerdotal status, especially in Judaism and Christianity. Interpreted in the broader sense, the priest shares many qualities with other types of religious functionaries, specialists, sacred persons, and holders of religious authority which have been recorded in the long religious history of the human race. Today, historians of religions acknowledge various categories of religious leadership: founder of a religion, reformer, prophet, seer, diviner, teacher, saint, priest, shaman, medicine man, witch doctor, etc., even though it is readily acknowledged that their functions sometimes overlap.

There are various perspectives for the study of religious leadership. Historians of Judaism, Christianity, Hinduism, or Buddhism for example, would attempt to articulate the meaning of the priesthood as understood by their respective religious communities. On the other hand, scholars of the history of religions (also known as comparative religions, or the general science of religions), which aims at an understanding of the religious history of the human race as a whole, would delineate the general meaning of religious leadership in the entire history of religions. In so doing, however, historians of religions are not unaware of the uniqueness of each religious tradition.

For the most part, historians of religions accept three presuppositions about man: (1) the fact of the eternally human, that is, men and women of all ages and ethnic backgrounds share the common quality of being human; (2) the fact of human corporateness, that is, man exists as man-in-society-and-culture; and (3) the fact of universal human need for salvation or enlightenment. Historians of religions also assume that all religions have three dimensions: (a) theoretical: e.g., symbol, concept, doctrine, dogma; (b) practical: e.g., cultus, worship, prayer, meditation; and (c) sociological: e.g., religious community, cult association, and various types of religious leadership, sacerdotal or otherwise.

The beginnings of religious leadership are clouded in the mist of prehistory. Many scholars assume that there was a time when people experienced a unity of the various dimensions of life which are now seen separately, as, for example, economics, art, and religion. Once upon a time, so writes Gerardus van der Leeuw: "Song was prayer; drama was divine performance; dance was cult."[1] Thus, in early pre-civilized societies there was no need for special religious functionaries as such, because all members participated in group activities which were religious and nonreligious simultaneously. Gradually, however, as prehistoric men advanced from the stage of food-gathering to hunting and fishing and to that of agriculture, they developed various forms of hunting or fertility cults that were performed by special individuals who could invoke supernatural power in controlling weather, charming animals, or healing the sick. It must have taken a long time, however, before the cultic functionaries became recognized as such.

We learn from archaeologists that agriculture and stock breeding developed as early as the eighth millenium B.C. in the Iranean Plateau. This marked the beginning of the so-called "food-producing revolution," which stimulated the rise of self-sustaining villages. The transition from the neolithic village pattern to a more advanced phase of the city and state was a long process. Around 3500 B.C., the first great civilization emerged in the Mesopotamian plain. Soon other civilizations arose in Egypt, Crete, India, China, Mexico, Peru, and Palestine. All these civilizations were based on fairly large societies with centralized authority, elaborate culture, organized cults, rituals, symbols, and various types of religious leadership. Probably the earliest significant religious leader ever recorded was the king, like those of ancient Egypt and China. The king was not a religious genius, but he was the instrument of divine power. In fact, the Egyptian king was not only the one recognized priest of all the gods, but was considered as one of the gods. Thus, when the Egyptian said that "the king was Horus, he did not mean that the king was playing the part of Horus, he meant that the king *was* Horus, that the god was effectively present in the king's body during the particular activity in question."[2] At the same time, it was taken for granted that regardless of who might bring sacrifice, every sacrifice was really offered by the king, who was the priest par excellence.

In some of the ancient civilizations the king delegated parts of his functions to the priests and the magistrates. This was the case with the priests in the Old and Middle Kingdoms in Egypt. In ancient Rome, the king divided his triple dignities—as judge, as priest, and as commander of the army—between the consuls and the *rex sacrorum*. Likewise, in ancient Greece, specialists in religion were recognized side by side with the magistrates as offices needed for the preservation of harmony and good order. Thus, after listing the duties of the civil magistrates, Aristotle writes in his *Politics:*

Another set of officers is concerned with the maintenance of religion; priests and guardians see to the preservation and repair of the temples of the gods and to other matters of religion. One office of this sort may be enough in small places, but in larger ones there are a great many besides the priesthood; for example, superintendents of public worship, guardians of shrines, treasurers of the sacred revenues. Nearly connected with these there are also the officers appointed for the performance of the public sacrifice, except any which the law assigns to the priests. . . . They are sometimes called archons, sometimes kings, and sometimes prytanes.[3]

In other civilizations the priest even competed with the king or overshadowed the throne. The most extreme case was Tibet where the Dalai Lama ruled as the *de facto* divine king until recent years. According to Georges Dumezil, the early Indo-European societies in India, Persia, and Europe were characterized by a hierarchically ordered, tripartite social strata—those of priests, warriors, and cultivator-herdsmen. The most important among the three was the stratum of priests, which was charged with sacral functions as much as the maintenance of juridical sovereignty.[4] Subsequently, Indian society developed the four main castes and numerous subcastes. Chief among them was the priestly caste called the Brahman; it enjoyed a virtual monopoly of religious functions but never attained political power.

Historically, as stated above, the priest often inherited or shared many of the functions of other types of religious leaders. For example, in ancient Rome, where the erection of bridges was considered a sacred act, the term *pontifex* meant "builder of bridges," signifying that the priests originated from primitive engineers who applied "bridge medicine."[5] We are also told that the Cananite word which meant "priest" in Ugaritic *(khn)* and in Hebrew *(kōhēn)*, signified "inspired soothsayer" *(kāhin)* among the ancient Arabs.[6] In some cases priests are "called" by God as individuals, while in other cases priests come from hereditary priestly families, classes, or tribes. The training for the priesthood also varies greatly according to different religious traditions. While the priesthood is often associated with sacrifice, an important act of mediation between men and the divine being, such an understanding of the priesthood is not applicable to those religions which do not believe in offering sacrifice.

Even this brief discussion demonstrates two major problems in defining the priesthood as we find it in the history of religions. First, those who are designated as priests in various religious traditions have been engaged in such a wide spectrum of activities that it is difficult to pinpoint the unique character of the priesthood. Second, in some religious traditions there are those who are not so designated but act as though they were priests; e.g., the *imām* in Islam and the *rabbi* in Judaism. Nevertheless, it is safe to conclude that various types of religious leadership are involved in some kinds of priestly functions, and that the religious community itself may be characterized by its priestly nature. Thus, by examining some of the classical forms of priesthood in contrast to other types of religious leadership in various religious communities, we may delineate certain general characteristics. In this task, we depend heavily on Joachim Wach's concept of the classical. Wach insists that this concept is not based on reduction from the wealth of the historical data; rather, he states: "The phenomena which we designate as classical represent something typical; they convey with regard to religious life and experience more than would be conveyed by an individual instance."[7] Following this insight, we will attempt to select a few classical forms of priesthood that we find in the history of religions.

In the so-called primitive religious communities, Robert Lowie astutely depicts the nature of a classical form of priesthood by comparing it with that of the shaman or medicine man. According to his observation, a shaman acquires his status through a personal communication from supernatural beings, whereas "the priest need not have this face-to-face relationship with the spirit world but must have competence in conducting ritual."[8] In other words, "Shamans are essentially mediums, for they are the mouthpieces of spirit beings. Priests are intermediaries between people and the spirits to whom they wish to address themselves."[9] While there are such exceptions as the inspired priests of Tonga who speak for the god or gods in the first person, in the main, ecstasy is not associated with the priest. Unlike the shaman or the medicine man who operates according to the influence of the spirit, the priest in the primitive religious communities stands for the ordered manifestation of the divine power in fixed times and places.[10]

In Hindu tradition, the priesthood is invariably understood in terms of caste. That is to say, Hinduism, which affirms that every aspect of life is ultimately determined by and related to the eternal cosmic law *(dharma)*, accepts the caste system as a part of the cosmic hierarchical structure. Historically, as early as the sixth century B.C. there was a hereditary priestly class or caste, even though the practice of priestly functions was not restricted to the Brahmans, the members of the priestly caste. The main priestly functions were the carrying out of the great sacrifices and the domestic rites. In the course of time the Brahmans developed the ten great divisions and many more subdivisions, some of which include nonpriestly activities. Nevertheless, the sacramental view of the universe which has sustained Hinduism throughout the ages acknowledges the prerogatives and duties of the priestly caste. At the same time, the sacramental view also recognizes that all men's work is sacrifice. Accordingly, as Coomaraswamy points out, Hinduism affirms that "every function, from that of the priest and the king down to that of the potter and scavenger, is literally a priesthood, and every operation a rite."[11] In short, the ideal of Hinduism is to keep in balance the unique place of the priestly caste and the priesthood of all members.

The so-called priesthood in Buddhism has undergone many phases of change historically. As E. J. Thomas once stated, the Buddhist movement began originally "not with a body of doctrine, but with the formation of a society bound by certain rules."[12] Early Buddhism took it for granted that the four subgroups—monks *(bhikkhu)*, nuns *(bhikkunī)*, laymen *(upāsaka)*, and laywomen *(upāsika)*—constituted the Buddhist community. Soon the Buddhist community came to be divided along the cultic and doctrinal lines into Theravāda (the tradition of the Elders), Mahāyāna (the Great Vehicle) and Esoteric (Tantric) traditions. In the Theravāda tradition, which was established in South and Southeast Asia, the monastic communities became all-powerful, whereby the *bhikkhu* came to be regarded not only as monks striving for their own enlightenment but also as priests in the sense of conducting liturgies, preaching and teaching for the spiritual welfare of the laity. In the Mahāyāna and Esoteric traditions, which penetrated East Asia, the monastics and the laity were understood to share the same path of the Buddha with different functions within the Buddhist community. And since the Mahāyāna and Esoteric traditions developed rich pantheons, the monastics took on full priestly functions, such as offering incantations addressed to the Buddhist deities and reading scriptures for every conceivable occasion.

It is interesting to note that both China and Japan developed multireligious systems which were patronized as well as controlled by the respective governments. In China, Confucianism, Taoism, and Bud-

dhism were seen as three facets of the same truth. Taoism and Buddhism had elaborate systems of priesthood serving the religious needs,
in a technical sense of the term, of the people. Equally important are
the nonecclesiastical priestly functions of (a) the Emperor as the Son of
Heaven and the head of the national family; (b) the head of the
household who was held responsible for family cults, especially in reference to the veneration of the ancestors; and (c) the literati *(Ju)* who
were charged to transmit the sacred traditions of the past to the present
and the future generations. The significance of the nonecclesiastical
priestly functions in China was eloquently described by Confucius in his
statement about the literati *(Ju)* as follows:

A *Ju* lives with the moderns but studies with the ancients. What he does today
will become an example for those in the generations to follow. When he lives
in times of political chaos, he neither courts favors from those in authority, nor
is boosted by those below. . . . Although he lives in danger, his soul remains his
own, and even then he does not forget the sufferings of the people.[13]

In Japan, Buddhism, the indigenous Shinto (the Way of the *kami* or
gods), and to a certain extent Confucianism, constituted a multireligious
system. The uniqueness of Japanese religious tradition was its acceptance of the sacredness of the national community, which was reigned
over by the imperial family by virtue of its solar ancestry.[14] Thus, the
emperor was regarded as Goth the manifest *kami* and the chief priest,
to whom the Shinto and Buddhist priests were subservient.

We cannot adequately deal with the checkered history of the Jewish
religious leadership. It is interesting to note, however, that the earliest
priests were primarily guardians of the sanctuary and its treasures; they
had nothing to do with sacrifices, which were offered by Noah,
Abraham, Jacob, and other patriarchs. Meanwhile, Israelite priesthood
gradually developed from a popular to a royal priesthood, which was an
uneasy fusion between the tradition of the Yahwist Levites and the
ancient pagan tradition of the "sons of Aaron." Later biblical legislation
recognized that only the priests had the prerogative of offering sacrifice
in the Temple; they were also entrusted with the Torah. Probably the
most striking phenomenon recorded in the biblical accounts is the
tension between the two types of religious leadership—the priest and
the prophet. What we learn from the utterances of Hosea, Isaiah, and
Jeremiah, for example, is not only the corrupt state of the priesthood,
which was no doubt true, but the fact that the priest and the prophet
had different kinds of calling. "The priest stands for the ordered, the
prophet . . . for the occasional representation of power and of mankind."[15] Interestingly enough, the effort to homologize the prophetic

and priestly ideals, as recorded in Deuteronomy, found its actual embodiment in the person of Ezekiel, who was both a priest and a prophet. After the rebuilding of the Temple the chief priest gained prominence in national life, but with the destruction of the Temple by the Romans the priesthood virtually lost all its influence among the Jews in the Diaspora. In its stead the legitimation of the rabbinate as another type of religious leadership took place, especially after the establishment of a fixed curriculum for the rabbis by the Mesopotamian and Palestinian academies.[16]

The priesthood in the Christian tradition is an important facet of the development of religious leadership in the religious history of the human race. An intriguing question to ask is how early Christianity, which had no living Jewish model of the priesthood, came to make frequent use of such symbolic expressions as those of the sacrifice and the high priest in explanation of the role of Christ in the New Testament. Moreover, all believers are said to share Christ's high priesthood (Ephesians 2:18), and the Church as his body is to be understood in terms of a royal priesthood (1 Peter 2:5; Revelation 5:10). Probably Christianity, which began as an apocalyptic sect within Judaism, shared the agony of the Jews over the loss of the Temple of Jerusalem in A.D. 70, and interpreted the life of Jesus and his community by idealizing and appropriating the symbols of the Temple priesthood and the sacrifice. On the other hand, early Christianity in the Hellenistic world, living as it was surrounded by the mystery cults, expressed its beliefs in terms of the myth of the hero, initiation rites, baptism, and sacred meal, all of which were ingredients of its cultural climate.[17] Then, with the development of the clerical hierarchy and of eucharistic theology, the office of the presbyter, which in early Christianity had no priestly connotations, came to be interpreted in sacerdotal terms based on the principle of participation in Christ's priesthood. The Protestant reformers, however, rejected the model of Levitical priesthood for the clergy and stressed the priesthood of all believers.

Among all the major religions of the world, Islam, which began both as a religion and an empire simultaneously, never developed ecclesiastical offices comparable to the priesthood in other religious traditions. Also, it is to be noted that there is no office that succeeds the prophethood of Muhammad. On the other hand, it was assumed that any public religious rite was to be led by the chief of the community, and the name *imām* (leader in prayer) was applied to the sovereign who conducted services in the mosque in the capital. With the expansion of Islam and the increase of mosques and the *salāt* (public prayer), it became customary for the local congregations to appoint the *imām* and also the *khatīb* (preacher) if there was a Friday sermon. Neither one is a sacerdotal office, however. Nevertheless, it was taken for granted that the whole Islamic community, called *Ummah*, was nothing short of a soteriological community, and that all aspects of the life of the Muslims were guided by the holy law *(Sharī'a)*.

In retrospect, it becomes evident that there is no simple definition of the term "priesthood," because its functions vary greatly according to different times and different religious traditions. It is also significant to note that there is a major religion like Islam which does not recognize any kind of sacerdotal office, and that in Chinese tradition the literati historically played a nonecclesiastical priestly role. Also, the kingship in many cultures had the dimension of the chief priest. The most fascinating lesson we learn from the history of religions is the soteriological character of the religious community as such, which is often expressed in terms of the "priesthood of all believers." All offices of religious leaders and functionaries, including the priesthood, are legitimatized by their respective religious communities, which ultimately play the priestly role of mediating between concrete human existence and the sacral reality, no matter how it is called. In this sense, the community, such as the Islamic Ummah, Buddhist Samgha, and Christian Ecclesia, is not simply a society of like-minded people. Throughout history, religious man has known that community "is something not manufactured, but given. . . . It need be founded upon no conviction, since it is evident. We do not become members of it, but 'belong to it.' "[18] Only in this context can the priesthood and other types of religious leadership be properly understood.

NOTES

1. G. van der Leeuw, *Sacred and Profane Beauty: the Holy in Art*, trans. David E. Green (New York: Holt, Rinehart & Winston, 1963), p.11.

2. H. and H. A. Frankfort, et al., *The Intellectual Adventure of Ancient Man* (Chicago: University of Chicago Press, 1946), pp. 64–65.

3. *Great Books of the Western World*, 9. *Aristotle: II* (Chicago: Encyclopaedia Britannica, Inc., 1952), p. 526.

4. Cf. Georges Dumezil, *Les dieux des Indo-Européens* (Paris: Presses Universaires de France, 1952); and *L'ideologie tripartie des Indo-Européens* (Brussels: Latomus, 1958).

5. G. van der Leeuw, *Religion in Essence and Manifestation*, trans. J. E. Turner (London: George Allen & Unwin, 1938), p. 219.

6. James Hastings, ed., *Encyclopaedia of Religion and Ethics*, vol. 10 (New York: Charles Scribner's Sons, 1951), p. 307.

7. Joachim Wach, *Types of Religious Experience: Christian and Non-Christian* (Chicago: University of Chicago Press, 1951), p. 51.

8. Cited in William A. Lessa and Evon Z. Vogt, *Reader in Comparative*

Religion: An Anthropological Approach (Evanston: Row, Peterson and Co., 1958), p. 413.

9. Ibid., p. 411.

10. G. van der Leeuw, op. cit., p. 219.

11. Ananda K. Coomaraswamy, *Hinduism and Buddhism* (New York: Philosophical Library, 1943), p. 27.

12. E. J. Thomas, *The History of Buddhist Thought* (New York: Barnes & Noble, 1933), p. 14.

13. Lin Yutang, ed. and trans., *The Wisdom of Confucius* (New York: Random House, 1938), p. 6.

14. See J. M. Kitagawa, "The Japanese *Kokutai:* History and Myth," *History of Religions,* vol. 13, no. 3 (February, 1974), pp. 209–26.

15. G. van der Leeuw, op. cit., p. 219.

16. Max Weber, *Ancient Judaism,* trans. and ed. Hans H. Gerth and Don Martindale (Glencoe: The Free Press, 1952), pp. 391–400.

17. Norman Perrin, *The New Testament: An Introduction* (New York: Harcourt Brace Jovanovich, 1974), pp. 41 and 51.

18. G. van der Leeuw, op. cit., p. 243.

chapter 6

THE PRIESTHOOD OF CHRIST

Myles M. Bourke

Any discussion of the priesthood of Christ in the New Testament is, of course, principally a discussion of the Epistle to the Hebrews. Perhaps at the time when Hebrews was written there was already in the Christian Church a fairly widespread current of thought which conceived of Jesus as priest; I do not think so, but the suggestive work of Gerd Theissen, which supports that view, cannot be set aside without serious consideration.[1] Briefly, Theissen's thesis is that the First Epistle of Clement and the letter of Ignatius to the Philadelphians show that the authors of each drew on a common tradition about the priesthood of Jesus which the author of Hebrews set himself to correct, not, indeed, by denying that priesthood, but by locating it solely in the cross, and by attacking the "mystery-piety" of the tradition that made Jesus the high priest of the Church's Eucharist. Regardless of the outcome of that discussion, it cannot be questioned that Hebrews, whether a corrective of an existing tradition or, on the contrary, the source of the development found in First Clement, is the fullest treatment of Jesus' priesthood available to us in early Christian literature.

I should like to deal with three aspects of the epistle, each of them important for the topic: (1) the union of a high Christology and an unusual emphasis on Jesus' humanity; (2) the view that the locus of Christ's sacrifice was not only the cross, but the cross and what the author calls the heavenly tabernacle; and (3) the conception that that sacrifice is a present offering of the exalted Christ. While there is general agreement that the first is an undeniable element of the epistle, many scholars think either that the other two are quite absent or that their presence is doubtful. In my opinion, all three are to be found in Hebrews, and all must be taken into account if one is to grasp the writer's understanding of Jesus' priesthood.

55

HIGH CHRISTOLOGY AND EMPHASIS
ON HUMANITY

The sonship of Jesus is presented in a manner which is, at first, puzzling. On the one hand, Jesus is the pre-existent Son of God. What had been said of divine wisdom is said of him: he is the "refulgence" *(apaugasma)* of the Father's glory; he bears the "very stamp" *(character)* of the Father's nature (Hebrews 1:3; cf. Wisdom 7:26); through him God created the world (Hebrews 1:2). In the ensuing comparison between the Son and the angels, the author of Hebrews does not hesitate to apply to him the address of the psalmist to God: "Thou, Lord, didst found the earth in the beginning, and the heavens are the work of thy hands" (Hebrews 1:10; cf. Psalms 102:25). At the same time, Jesus' identification with those he came to save is a constant theme of the epistle. "It was fitting that he, for whom and by whom all things exist, in bringing many sons to glory, should make the pioneer of their salvation perfect through suffering. . . . Since therefore the children share in flesh and blood, he himself likewise partook of the same nature" (Hebrews 2:10, 14).

It is this oneness of Jesus with his brethren that enables him to become their high priest: "Therefore he had to be made like his brethren in every respect, so that he might become a merciful and faithful high priest in the service of God, to make expiation for the sins of the people" (Hebrews 2:17). "Flesh," the designation of man in his weakness—that existence the Son shared. The days of his mortal life are called "the days of his flesh": "In the days of his flesh, Jesus offered up prayers and supplications, with loud cries and tears, to him who was able to save him from death. . . . Although he was a Son, he learned obedience through what he suffered; and being made perfect he became the source of eternal salvation to all who obey him" (Hebrews 5:7–9). As pre-existent Son he is still such in "the days of his flesh"; the author in no way supports the curious notion of a kenosis in which the entrance of the pre-existent Son into the fullness of man's existence involves his ceasing to be what he had been. Yet his humanity must be drawn into the fullness of the divine life, and the author can say that it was only after suffering and death had been experienced by the human Jesus that he became Son of God; the words of Psalms 2:7, "Thou art my Son, today I have begotten thee" are addressed to him at his exaltation in Hebrews 1:5.

These two aspects of Jesus' sonship are indeed in a certain tension, but one which does not defy resolution. As certain as the author is of Jesus' pre-existence as Son, he is also certain that his humanity was no sham. It was, on the contrary, the means whereby he was able to show that perfect obedience by which true sonship is proved. He entered fully into the human condition, and he became, as man, both Son of God and high priest. For his obedience consisted supremely in his total devotion to the Father, even unto death. "A body thou hast prepared for me" (Hebrews 10:5). These words of the Septuagint version of Psalms 40[39]:7 are placed by the author on the lips of the incarnate Son as he enters the world. "Then I said, 'Lo, I have come to do thy will, O God'. . . . And by that will we have been sanctified through the offering of the body of Jesus Christ once for all" (Hebrews 10:7, 10). He who became like his brethren in every respect (Hebrews 2:17) did so that by his obedience unto death he might lead them out of their alienation from God into his own new life. There is only one thing in which his human life differed from theirs—yet what a difference! "We have not a high priest who is unable to sympathize with our weaknesses, but one who in every respect has been tempted as we are, yet without sinning" (Hebrews 4:15).

In his valuable study, *The Humanity and Divinity of Christ,* John Knox struggles at length with the concept of Jesus' sinlessness, and says: "The point which I have been trying to make in all this is that while this author to the Hebrews cannot bring himself to speak, or even to think, of Jesus as a sinner (any more than we can), nevertheless his whole understanding of the story of the Christ and of the role of the human Jesus in it logically requires that the latter should have shared completely in our human lot—without any reservation at all, even this one."[2] It seems to me that Knox does not give sufficient weight to the other side of the picture which the author of Hebrews has drawn: Jesus, the pre-existent Son, whose closeness to the Father is such that sin in him is utterly inconceivable. He can and does share man's existence in its fullness; that is, so to speak, the stuff of his sacrifice. But there is one point in which he cannot be like his brethren; namely, in their rebellion against God. "Lo, I have come to do your will"; it is under the sign of obedience, however painfully learned, that the whole human life of the Son of God is lived. And, in fact, it is only such a perfectly obedient one who is able to lead his sinful brethren out of their bondage to sin: "It was fitting that we should have such a high priest, holy, blameless, unstained, separated from sinners, exalted above the heavens" (Hebrews 7:26).

THE LOCUS OF CHRIST'S SACRIFICE

While the entire earthly life of Jesus was one of perfect obedience, it is only his death which Hebrews interprets in terms of sacrifice. Does that interpretation mean that the author regarded Jesus' death and his sacrifice as conterminous, and the exaltation of the crucified one merely

as the sequel to his completed sacrifice? An affirmative answer to that
question is given by many scholars. I think that the answer, so far from
being correct, is based in some instances on a mistaken notion of Old
Testament sacrifice, and in others on an ignoring of the way in which
the author applies Old Testament sacrificial concepts to the redemptive
work of Jesus.

It is obviously impossible to attempt here to give an adequate treatment of sacrifice in the Old Testament. But it is generally agreed by
students of the subject that the slaughter of the animal victim was by
no means the principal part of the sacrifice. The animal was slaughtered
in order that its blood might be released. The blood was the element
in which life was thought to reside (Leviticus 17:11, 14); as the bearer
of life it had a sacred, a divine quality. By reason of its sacred character,
when poured out on the altar or sprinkled on the place of expiation the
blood was an effective symbol of purification of sin and of the re-estab-
lishment of union between God and man which had been broken by sin.
As W. D. Davies puts it: "By the outpouring of the blood, life was
released, and in offering this to God the worshipper believed that the
estrangement between him and the Deity was annulled, or that the
defilement which separated them was cleansed."[3] We may pass over
the question whether it is accurate to say that the blood ritual was
regarded precisely as an "offering." Whatever view is held on that,
there is no doubt that the ritual was the essential element of the sacrifice, for the atoning power of the sacrifice was attributed to the blood
manipulation: "The life of the creature is in the blood, and I direct you
to place it upon the altar, to make atonement for you; for it is the blood
that makes atonement, by reason of the life" (Leviticus 17:11).

Even with due regard given to those considerations, it might still
seem possible to hold that Jesus' sacrifice was simply his death on the
cross. For was it not there that his blood was poured out, and that
atonement took place? But the picture drawn in Hebrews applies the
blood ritual to Jesus' sacrifice in a way that goes beyond his death. In
the ninth chapter of the epistle the author makes a comparison between the sacrificial worship of the Old Covenant and that of the
New, and contrasts principally the sacrificial activity of the Hebrew
high priest and the sacrifice of Jesus. He speaks of the "earthly sanctuary," the Mosaic tabernacle, with its two parts: the "outer" tabernacle
into which the ordinary priests entered continually to perform their
ritual duties; and the "second" tabernacle, behind the veil, into which
the high priest alone entered, and that but once a year, with the blood
"which he offered for himself and for the errors of the people" (Hebrews 9:7). The high priestly ritual there referred to is, of course, the
ritual of the Day of Atonement (cf. Leviticus 16:1–16). On that day,

the blood of the animal victims was sprinkled directly on, and in front of, the propitiatory which was over the ark of the covenant (Exodus 25:17–22).

This entrance of the high priest into the holy of holies with the sacrificial blood, and the blood sprinkling within that inner tabernacle, is the Old Testament model which the author of Hebrews uses in his portrayal of the sacrifice of Jesus. But the contrast between the high priest of the Old Covenant and Jesus is not only the enormous difference in the blood which was brought in, but that the sanctuary of the Old Covenant was an earthly sanctuary. The expiation there effected could never cleanse the conscience of the worshippers (Hebrews 9:9, 14), the ritual was only "a shadow of the good things to come" (Hebrews 10:1). "But when Christ appeared as high priest of the good things that have come, . . . he entered once for all into the sanctuary, . . . not with the blood of goats and calves, but with his own blood, and achieved eternal redemption" (Hebrews 9:11–12). The sanctuary into which Jesus entered was no earthly one: "Christ did not enter into a sanctuary made by hands, a mere copy of the true one, but into heaven itself, that he might appear before God now on our behalf" (Hebrews 9:24).

The heavenly sanctuary where Jesus' sacrifice is brought to completion is the "true" one, in contrast to the earthly sanctuary of the Old Covenant. The conception that the earthly sanctuary reflects a heavenly model has both biblical and Platonic origins. Moses was commanded to construct the tabernacle according to the model shown to him by God (Exodus 25:9–40). But although the idea was certainly a Semitic one, it is paralleled in the Platonic conception that all earthly reality is simply a shadow of the "true" heavenly world. The affinity of the epistle with the thought-world of Alexandrian Judaism suggests that it is the Platonic influence that is dominant here. In any case, what is important for the question of the locus of Jesus' sacrifice is that Hebrews portrays that sacrifice as coming to its completion not on earth but in the heavenly world. No matter how important the cross is, one cannot take the extended comparison of Hebrews 9 seriously without realizing that the author does not make Jesus' sacrifice end with his death. Just as the Day of Atonement cannot be conceived of except as including the blood sprinkling in the holy of holies, so it is impossible to regard Jesus' entrance into the heavenly sanctuary as the consequence of his sacrifice completed on the cross, rather than as part of that sacrifice which began on earth and reached its climax in heaven with Jesus' exaltation. Since the author draws an exact parallel between the entrance of the high priest into the inner tabernacle, and the entrance of Jesus into heaven, it is difficult to see how F. F. Bruce can say: "There have been expositors who, pressing the analogy of the Day of Atonement beyond the limits observed by our author, have argued that the expiatory work of Christ was not completed on the cross . . ."[4] The limits observed are precisely the reason why one must look for the heavenly counterpart of the high priest's sprinkling of the blood, which was not a sequel to the sacrifice but an essential part of it. Hebrews conceives Jesus' sacrifice as spanning earth and heaven. It is only with his exaltation and entrance into the heavenly sanctuary that he "achieved eternal redemption" (Hebrews 9:12).[5]

THE PERMANENCE OF THE SACRIFICE

Does the author of Hebrews think that the once accomplished sacrifice is now over? There are certainly some texts which seem to say that he does (e.g. Hebrews 10:12), and the constantly repeated insistence upon the "once-for-all" and definitive nature of the sacrifice (Hebrews 9:12, 26, 28; 10:10) have been taken as ruling out any interpretation which would see the sacrifice as a present reality. The heavenly intercession of the exalted Jesus (Hebrews 7:25) is commonly understood as a pleading before God of the merits of the eternally effective but past sacrifice. Yet there are other considerations which suggest a different conclusion.

When the author gives what he calls the "chief point" of his argument (Hebrews 8:1–2) it is that "we have such a high priest, one who is seated at the right hand of the throne of the Majesty in heaven, a minister in the sanctuary and the true tabernacle which is set up not by man but by the Lord." Is that undoubtedly present ministry of Jesus different from his sacrificial offering? Because of the way in which the author conceives the entrance of Jesus into the sanctuary as the climactic point of his sacrifice, it seems, on the contrary, that the present ministry of Jesus and the sacrificial offering are the same. An action completed in the earthly sphere would be an event of the past, but that is not so of one completed in the heavenly order. For one of the qualities of that order is its eternity. It is no accident that Hebrews, which insists on the heavenly character of the completed sacrifice of Jesus, is no less insistent on the eternity of his priesthood (Hebrews 6:20; 7:24).

To appreciate the force of that fact, I think that one must seriously consider the relation between the epistle and the thought-world of Alexandrian Judaism. Is it simply coincidental that Hebrews has so many points of contact with the writings of Philo? S. Sowers has claimed that "the writer of Heb. has come from the same school of Alexandrian Judaism as Philo, and . . . Philo's writings still offer us the best single body of *religionsgeschichtliche* material we have for this N.T. document."[6] In spite of the differences between Philo and Hebrews, mainly in respect to eschatology, there is good reason to agree with that opinion. It certainly offers a satisfactory solution to the problem of why there are in the epistle texts which speak of the eternity of Christ's priesthood and others which speak of his sacrifice as completed. Instead of being forced to conclude that the author conceives of Jesus as eternal high priest in every respect except the one which is central to priesthood, namely, the offering of sacrifice, one has a consistent picture of the eternal priest and his eternal offering. There is a comment of Philo which sheds much light on how the author of Hebrews conceived of the latter. Following the Platonic distinction of *aiōn* as timeless eternity and *chronos* as the successive time of this world, Philo says: "The true name of *aiōn* is 'today'."[7] Since Jesus' sacrifice comes to its completion in the heavenly sanctuary which belongs to the eternal order, that sacrifice, in its climactic moment, is not an event of the past but one which is present in the eternal "today." Obviously, the death of Jesus is a past event. If his sacrifice and his death were conterminous, there would be no possibility of conceiving the sacrifice as present, except in its enduring effect. But if it is impossible to find in Hebrews any such equivalence of sacrifice and death, and if the sacrifice begun on the cross comes to completion in the heavenly sanctuary, it seems impossible to take that depiction of the sacrifice seriously without admitting its eternal presence.

What, then, of the texts of Hebrews which appear to suggest, by insisting that it is completed and unrepeatable, that the sacrifice is over? One must, in the first place, recall the situation in which the author writes. He is contrasting the sacrifice of Christ with those of the Old Covenant, specifically with the annually repeated Day of Atonement sacrifices. The "once-for-all" nature of Jesus' sacrifice is asserted in contrast to those constantly repeated and ineffectual sacrifices which were simply a foreshadowing of his perfect self-offering. That Jesus' sacrifice is definitive does not mean that it took place once and is now over and done with, but rather that it is once-for-all and definitive because it is eternally present and eternally being presented to God.

Secondly, one must recognize that different images used in Hebrews overlap. To claim that such a text as Hebrews 10:12 precludes the present reality of Jesus' self-offering because he is there pictured as having completed his sacrifice and being seated in majesty, is to forget that the author wishes to claim that Jesus is not only priest but reigning messianic king. It is only when the images are taken as pointers to a temporal time sequence that they are mutually exclusive. To impose such a time sequence upon the thought of the epistle is to ignore the contrast which the author makes between the earthly and the heavenly order. For him, eternity is a quality of all heavenly reality. It is important to remember, of course, that while the author thinks in the same tradition as that in which Philo stood, he is faithful to the time sequence of Jewish eschatology. Thus, for him, the heavenly sanctuary existed eternally, but Jesus' sacrifice is eternal because what had begun on earth at a determined point of time was inserted into the heavenly order with the exaltation of the crucified one and his entrance into the heavenly sanctuary.

I am aware that the understanding of Christ's priesthood here presented is not without its difficulties, and a far more extensive study than this would be necessary if one wished to deal with them adequately. I believe, however, that it does represent the thought of the epistle. I should like to say, finally, that what the author of Hebrews wrote is not to be rejected out of hand as the remnant of a world view which the modern Christian cannot in any way share. Certainly, a translation of the epistle's images is necessary. But when the heavenly sanctuary is understood, not as a place beyond the clouds but as a symbol of the new existence which came to Jesus with his resurrection-exaltation, an existence which can be shared by those who believe in him and obey him, the epistle can still be a source of strength and nourishment for the Church of today.

NOTES

1. Gerd Thiessen, *Untersuchungen zum Hebräerbrief* (Gütersloh, West Germany: Gütersloher Verlagshaus, 1969).

2. John Knox, *The Humanity and Devinity of Christ* (Cambridge: At the University Press, 1967), p. 49.

3. W. D. Davies, *Paul and Rabbinic Judaism*, 2nd ed. (London: S.P.C.K., 1958), p. 235.

4. F. F. Bruce, *The Epistle to the Hebrews* (Grand Rapids: Eerdmans, 1964), p. 200.

5. As will be evident, this translation takes the Greek aorist participle of the verse as an aorist of contemporaneous action.

6. S. Sowers, *The Hermeneutics of Philo and Hebrews* (Richmond: John Knox Press, 1965), p. 66.

7. Philo, *De fuga*, no. 57, Loeb Classical Library, vol. 5, p. 40.

chapter 7

PRIESTHOOD IN THE NEW TESTAMENT

Louis Weil

The New Testament does not answer all the questions the Church asks about the nature of the ordained priesthood. Holy Scripture does not supply us with even a rudimentary liturgical form for ordination, nor does it offer a clear structure for holy orders, nor a developed rationale for such designated office within the life of the Church. Rather, what the New Testament does offer, and what is critically important to our developing concept of ministry—whether ordained or lay—is an expression of the underlying phenomenon of particularized office within the Body of Christ.

The New Testament Church acted under the imperative of its experience of the risen Lord and the outpouring of the power of the Holy Spirit. This action was often spontaneous, as the early community found itself obliged to deal with new situations. The regularization of the structures of office, the normative designation of persons to perform specific ministries within the Church's life, was to come later as the need arose for the clarification of responsibility and authority. During the earliest stages, as the New Testament makes evident, such regularization had not yet emerged. Rather, the Church dealt with its internal life and its mission to the world with flexible means, living in the hope of the immediate return of Christ.

It was out of such a flexible framework, however, that a normative pattern began to form. Long before the Church became an institutionalized force in secular society, with the implicit acknowledgement that the Second Coming was not imminent and that the Church was probably here to stay for a while, a threefold pattern for the ordained ministry had come to be generally accepted. It was a structure which emerged under the guidance of the Spirit and was rooted in the New Testament evidence. Thus it is fair to suggest that although the ministry as it later developed was generated out of the early Church's zeal to do the work given it by God, the New Testament itself knows of no cultic Christian priesthood, no clearly designated office of sacerdotal responsibility. It will be the purpose of this essay to delineate, in a rudimentary way, what the New Testament does suggest about the ordained ministry and more particularly about the ordained priesthood.

It has often been noted that the New Testament does not employ a priestly vocabulary in speaking of those who minister in the Church. The New Testament never applies the Greek word *hiereus* (priest) to the men and women who minister, but only to Christ. Since by the close of the second century the word came to be so applied, we must attempt to see what insight the emergence of this vocabulary gives us into the relation which the Church saw to exist between the ministry of its designated officers and the priestly work of Christ.[1] When the New Testament speaks of priesthood, it is either in regard to that of Christ or else to that of God's people, as in the celebrated passage in which the Church is addressed as "a chosen race, a royal priesthood, a consecrated nation, a people set apart to sing the praises of God." (1 Peter 2:9) The latter is the priesthood of a holy life to which all Christians are called by virtue of their baptism; it is the life of holiness like that to which the Jewish people saw priests to be called.[2] This priesthood of God's people is not to be confused with the ministerial priesthood. The priesthood of the Church is not expressed primarily in regard to cultic worship, but rather in its corporate life of holiness. Tillard notes that the "spiritual sacrifices" which God's people are called to offer are not to be understood as ritual acts. He continues:

To see in the "royal priesthood" the power which every Christian possesses by the very fact of his baptism to take an active part in the ritual cult and especially in the eucharist as a fully accredited member, is to falsify the thought of the text. Here we are in another setting, that of holiness of life. This holiness derives from Christ. Rather than being a matter of participation in the priesthood of Christ, it is much more a matter of the effect of that priesthood, of its repercussion in and through the life of Christians.[3]

A failure to distinguish between the priesthood of the Church and that of the ministerial priesthood—a classical problem of Reformation theology—can only obscure the special role of the ordained ministry in the service of the whole Church. It is because of the unique priesthood of Christ that the Church is able to offer spiritual sacrifices which are acceptable to God since, as the author of the Epistle to the Hebrews writes, "the blood of Christ, who offered himself as the perfect sacrifice to God through the eternal Spirit, can purify our inner self from dead actions so that we do our service to the living God" (Hebrews 9:14). The role of the ordained ministry, as it emerges from the New Testament documents, is to serve God's people in the building up of the body, to teach and to celebrate the signs by which the faithful are perpetually renewed in their vocation.

Such a ministry of service, however, takes many diverse forms in the New Testament, nor are those forms always clearly distinguished between persons whom we would identify as ordained as contrasted with others not ordained. The New Testament gives evidence of various persons who assisted the apostles: Were they clergy or laity? In some instances their function was authorized by prayer and the laying on of hands. Such, for example, was the selection of seven men to assist the Twelve in some of the practical aspects of the ministry in Jerusalem. We read that the seven were presented to the apostles "who prayed and laid their hands on them" (Acts 6:6). Similarly in Antioch, the Holy Spirit indicated to the prophets of the Church there that Barnabas and Saul should be set apart for a special work. "So it was that after fasting and prayer they laid their hands on them and sent them off" (Acts 13:3).[4] Although these examples should not be interpreted as a fully developed rite of ordination, there can be no question that we see in them a clear action of designation for some specific work of ministry.

Yet there are other examples of persons who assisted the apostles and for whom there is no evidence of such ministerial designation. The last chapter of the Epistle to the Romans refers to the fact that Christians met in the home of Prisca and Aquila and also in the house of Gaius (Romans 16:5, 23). Again, in the Epistle to the Colossians, greeting is sent to the community which met in the home of Nympha. It would, of course, be foolish to make too much of such passages. Yet we do know that Christians normally met in private houses and there formed the nucleus of their community. The focus of such gatherings was the celebration of the Eucharist, "the breaking of bread" which characterized the life of the small fellowship from the beginning.[5] Although it is probably reasonable to suppose that when an apostle was present at such a gathering he would have presided and thus, in all likelihood, offered the eucharistic blessing over the bread and wine, it is nevertheless evident that given the itinerant lives of the apostles, many eucharistic gatherings took place at which no apostle was present. The New Testament evidence simply does not support the imposition of a fully developed system of "cultic delegation"—that is foreign to the very climate of the texts. In the absence of an apostle, perhaps the most likely person to have presided at the Eucharist would have been the host in whose home the faithful had gathered. Father Raymond Brown, the

distinguished Roman Catholic biblical scholar, has pointed out that
there is scarcely a hint in regard to this question in the New Testament.
The New Testament writings nowhere speak of the disciples, apostles,
or presbyter-bishops in regard to the presidential role in the Eucharist.
Rather, this role emerged gradually in the Church's life and fused with
other types of ministry.[6]

The office of liturgical presidency touches on one of the most significant dimensions of the development of the ordained priesthood in the
Church. There is nothing really surprising about the absence of a
priestly vocabulary in regard to the Christian ministry since, during the
time of the earliest years of the Church's life, the Jewish priesthood
remained intact, and there was no attempt on the part of the Church
to absorb the characteristics of that cultic ministry. The word 'priest'
was indelibly related to the Jewish cultic framework. Further, the celebration of the Eucharist, even allowing for its origin in the Passover
meal, or at least in a fellowship meal deeply imbued with the spirit of
the Passover, was not directly related to the Jewish priestly activity. It
is important for us to remember the twofold aspect of the Passover in
Jewish religious practice: First, the cultic or sacrificial act performed by
the priests involved the pouring out of the blood of the slain animal at
the foot of the altar.[7] The other aspect of the Passover was the meal
which commemorated God's saving act in the Exodus. This latter was
a family or fraternal meal, presided over by the father of the family or
the leader of the fellowship. As Tillard comments:

This second panel of the Passover diptych thus required no Levitical priestly
quality in the person presiding. The priestly act was antecedent to it. One can,
accordingly, understand that in the celebration of the Memorial of the Lord,
when the first Christians proclaimed that his Death had been the perfect and
unique Sacrifice, they were not spontaneously inclined to ascribe to the one
who presided the title or the character of 'priest'. The priestly quality of the
mystery thus 'commemorated' belonged, for them, as the Epistle to the Hebrews later made explicit, to the historical event of the death of Jesus and to
his entry into the sanctuary of God through his own blood.[8]

In this light it is easy to see why the early Church did not apply the
priestly vocabulary of the Jewish Levitical priesthood to the role of
liturgical leadership in its own eucharistic celebrations. The association
of such a vocabulary with Jewish sacrifices, which for Christians had
been fulfilled in the unique self-sacrifice of Christ, would have served
more to confuse than to proclaim their faith. It is the assertion of this
fulfillment which lies at the heart of the Epistle to the Hebrews.

Although the transition within the Church to the use of a priestly vocabulary in regard to the sacramental ministry lies outside the scope of this paper, it is relevant to our concern to note that this development seems to have come about under the influence of the institutions of the Old Testament. The first evidence we have comes from Tertullian, who, toward the end of the second century, uses a full priestly vocabulary when he writes of baptism and the ministers who perform it. Interestingly, his writing emphasizes the typological relationship between the Old Testament figures and their fulfillment in the Christian rites. What we see here is that the Christian community had come to understand its designated ministers as the fulfillment of those of the Old Testament, and thus, appropriately, to take up the priestly vocabulary associated with that cultic ministry. In his reference to laymen in the same treatise, Tertullian also brings before us the vivid distinction which had emerged in the Church's consciousness between those who are ordained and those who are not, and the normal responsibility of the former in regard to the sacramental actions.[9] In Tertullian's writing, the bishop is seen as the high priest *(summus sacerdos)*—the fullness of all priestly ministry, the one by whose authority all such ministry is performed.

The significance of this evolution for the Church's understanding of the Eucharist can hardly be exaggerated. Whereas, as we have noted, the Jews did not understand the Passover meal as a narrow priestly or sacrificial act, for Christians the Eucharist came increasingly to take on sacrificial significance. Its centrality in the Church's life as the *anamnesis* of Christ's sacrifice gave to those who presided over it a profound association with Christ's own sacrificial offering, and they came appropriately to be called "priests." In spite of the Levitical antecedents in Jewish religion, this Christian priesthood was a new thing, a ministry related to the unique priestly self-offering of Christ. Thus it may be seen truly to have its origins implicit in the New Testament documents. The Church lives in its celebration of the victory of Christ's death and resurrection: the Church was generated out of those events. The New Testament proclaims that mystery, and the faithful make explicit its abiding power in their continuing celebration of the Eucharist. The ordained priest in his presidential role carries a particularly powerful symbolic association with Christ himself.

The special relationship which exists between the ordained priest and the sacraments in terms of the "building up of the Body of Christ," although not explicitly developed in the New Testament writings, lies nevertheless beneath the phenomenon of the designated ministry as a fundamental dynamic. As we have already observed, the New Testament speaks of many different forms of ministry. Raymond Brown sees the antecedents of the priestly ministry as fourfold: the disciple, the apostle, the presbyter-bishop, and the celebrant.[10] In regard to the last of these, given the silence of the New Testament in regard to the presidential role, Brown writes of the regularization of the consent of the community for those who manifested this charism. Here we see the way in which ordination emerged naturally out of the experience of the young Church: there was an awareness that those who would act in the name of the apostles should receive some explicit sign of their relationship to the ministry of the apostles. Such a sign, rudimentary as it may have been in the earliest stages, was a natural act of the Church toward those who would minister from the very beginning. Whatever cultural or practical factors may have influenced the Church's understanding of the ordained ministry, it recognized the need "for specific, designated, empowered individuals in the body to assure the continuity of the authority and power of the risen Lord in the Church."[11] These individuals were seen to bear the authority of "holy order," a designated office bearing a particular relation to the life of the whole body, whatever particular form of ministry the person "in orders" might be called to fulfill.

Among the varied forms of ministry of which the New Testament speaks, there appear two fundamental underlying dynamics: *episcope* and *diakonia,* oversight and service. Not surprisingly, two forms of ministry emerged as particularly important from the New Testament period: episcopate and diaconate. These two forms of ministry serve to remind us of the two aspects of New Testament ministry: responsibility for the good of God's people, and faithfulness in their service. The acceptance of a priestly vocabulary did not contradict those underlying dynamics, but simply served to emphasize their relation to the priestly offering of Christ, who is himself the model and source of all ministry among his members.

NOTES

1. Cf. J. M. R. Tillard, "What Priesthood Has the Ministry?" *One in Christ* (1973), vol. 9, no. 3, pp. 237–269, where a detailed discussion of this question may be found.

2. Cf. J. H. Elliott, *The Elect and the Holy* (Leiden: E. J. Brill, 1966), p. 185, where it is indicated that the passage from 1 Pet can be interpreted only against its Old Testament background; cf. Lev 19:2; 21:8.

3. Tillard, op. cit., pp. 249–250.

4. Cf. similar examples in 1 Tim 4:14; 5:22; 2 Tim 1:6.

5. Cf. Acts 2:42.

6. R. E. Brown, *Priest and Bishop* (New York: Paulist/Newman Press, 1970), pp. 40 ff.

7. Roland de Vaux, *Ancient Israel: Its Life and Institutions* (New York: McGraw-Hill, 1965), vol. 2, pp. 484 ff.

8. Tillard, op. cit., p. 256.

9. *On Baptism*, 17:1–2.

10. R. E. Brown, op. cit., pp. 21–43.

11. William R. McCarthy, "The Three-fold Ministry and the Holy Spirit" (seminar paper presented at Nashotah House).

chapter 8

PRESBYTERS IN THE EARLY CHURCH

Massey H. Shepherd, Jr.

To avoid all confusion in this essay, it is necessary to remember that in the ancient languages of the Bible and early Christian literature the terms "presbyter" and "priest" are different words and refer to different functions of ministry. In English, however, the two terms are etymologically the same. The Latin *presbyter* was contracted in Anglo-Saxon to *prēost*, and in Middle English to *preest*.[1] One recalls John Milton's caustic comment in his sonnet "On the New Forcers of Conscience under the Long Parliament," after the Presbyterians in Parliament had abolished episcopacy: "New Presbyter is but old Priest writ large."

The ancient distinction of the two terms is preserved in the Episcopal Church, in that its canon law refers exclusively to the Order of Presbyters, whereas in the Book of Common Prayer the normative term for this order, with one exception, is that of Priest.[2] The proposed rites of ordination in *Services for Trial Use* (1970) have introduced the term "presbyter" in several rubrics, and in one instance in the text of the rite.[3]

Presbyter comes, by way of Latin from a Greek comparative adjective, also used substantively, meaning "an older one" or "elder." In its literal meaning the "elder" is contrasted with the "younger," not only in age but also in maturity of wisdom and experience.[4] In certain contexts, "elders" refers to those of ancient times who passed on their traditions.[5] More often the word denotes those who hold a specific office or ministry; and it is with this sense of the term that we are concerned here.

The model for Christian presbyters was the council of elders in the cities and towns where Jews were resident. Tradition derived their

71

origin from the appointment of elders by Moses, probably from the heads of families or clans.[6] In New Testament times the common names for these Jewish councils were *synedrion* ("a sitting together"; in Hebrew, *sanhedrin*), or *gerousia* ("a senate of old men"). Christian usage preferred the word *presbyterion*.[7] The chief body and final court of appeal of such councils was the great Sanhedrin in Jerusalem, often referred to in the Gospels and Acts. The ruling high priest presided over it, with the assistance of seventy members drawn from the chief priests, scribes (experts in the law), and elders.

These councils were self-perpetuating bodies with primarily judicial responsibility for interpreting what was "binding and loosing," what was or was not permissible according to the Law of the Old Testament. They acted as a collegial body, and no one member could make decisions without at least two others.[8] The elders had no official connection with the synagogues, for a synagogue could be formed by any group of ten Jewish males.[9] Yet it is reasonable to suppose that, as honored persons of the community, the elders would have prominent seats in the synagogues which they attended, or would be requested to read and interpret the Scriptures in the assemblies for worship; and they would be eligible for election by the synagogue congregation as its rulers *(archisynagogos)*.[10]

The Christian council of "apostles and elders," or of "James and the elders," in the early Jerusalem church appears analogous to the Jewish Sanhedrin. They made decisions about what was "binding and loosing" in the relations of Jewish and Gentile converts to the Church.[11] We are not told how these elders were appointed to assist the apostles. But in the mission churches, the Evangelist tells us that Paul and Barnabas appointed elders in the churches they founded in Galatia; and in the Pastoral Epistles, Titus is enjoined to "appoint elders in every town."[12] In his authentic letters, Paul never mentions presbyters. He refers to those who "lead," whether in admonishing or in laboring; but the context shows that he was concerned with example of life rather than with an office of ministry.[13]

In the scattered notices of presbyters in the literature of the post-apostolic age, their duties are variously indicated: having general oversight of their churches and guarding them from false teachers; and themselves preaching and teaching, ministering to the sick, and setting examples of service.[14] This brings us inevitably to the much debated question of the relation between presbyters and bishops in this early transitional period. Are these terms synonymous, referring only to differing functions of the same ministry, or are they always to be distinguished as separate offices of ministry?[15]

It is a curious fact, and a cause of differing interpretations of the origin of the episcopate, that in our sources prior to Ignatius of Antioch (martyred ca. 115), the references are either to "bishops and deacons" or to "presbyters." St. Paul, our earliest witness, in one instance addresses "bishops and deacons" in his Letter to the Philippians (1:1). This letter is a thank-you note to a church which had repeatedly given him material assistance; and it is likely that the bishops and deacons were responsible for gathering and sending it to him. In view of St. Paul's regard for charismatic gifts of ministry in his churches, it would be pressing the evidence too far to claim for these bishops and deacons at Philippi a ministry of leadership.[16]

Again, we must turn to the post-apostolic literature to gain some insight into the emerging leadership of bishops, with their assisting deacons. The *Didache* enjoins the churches to which it is addressed:

Appoint therefore for yourselves bishops and deacons worthy of the Lord, gentle men and not lovers of money, truthful and tested. For they also perform the liturgy [*lit.,* "liturgize the liturgy"] of the prophets and teachers. . . . They are your honored ones with the prophets and teachers.[17]

As in St. Paul, there is no mention of presbyters. The bishops and deacons have liturgical functions; but one detects, in the injunction "not lovers of money," a fiscal responsibility.

In the letter known as First Clement, written by the church in Rome (ca. 96) to the church in Corinth to protest the latter's removal of its ministers, we read:

They [the apostles] preached from district to district, and from city to city, and they appointed their first converts, testing them by the Spirit, to be bishops and deacons of future believers (42:4).

The letter goes on to remark that the apostles foresaw rivalry for the office of *episcope*, and therefore arranged that other "tested men" should succeed to their "liturgy":

We consider it unjust, therefore, to remove from the "liturgy" those who were appointed by them [the apostles] or by other eminent men,[18] with the consent of the whole church, and who have "liturgized" to the flock of Christ blamelessly, humbly, peaceably, and unselfishly, and so have had testimony by all for many years. For our sin is not small, if we cast out from the episcopate those who have blamelessly and holily offered the gifts.

The author then concludes with a comment that the presbyters of old, now dead, are blessed, for they have no fear that any will remove them from "their appointed place."[19]

As the late Walter Lowrie pointed out many years ago, a presbyter with an "appointed place" was a bishop—one in charge of the liturgy and its attendant dispensor of its offerings for those in need.[20] This does not preclude the fact that the bishop was a member, indeed the head, of the presbytery. This distinction does not contradict those passages where the juxtaposition of bishops and presbyters appears to make them synonymous.[21]

In the larger cities there would be several Christian congregations, just as there were many Jewish synagogues. These would be the result of evangelizing by different apostles or missionaries. In such places there would be, as in Jewish communities, a collegiate presbyterate; but each congregation might have had as its head a bishop. It was the threat to the unity of these congregations in the post-apostolic age, from both heresy within and persecution without, that led to a centralizing of authority in a single bishop. In smaller Christian communities, with only one congregation, there would be only one bishop in any case.

The process to monepiscopacy—one bishop in each city or town—is the burden of the letters of Bishop Ignatius of Antioch (ca. 115). Unity about the one bishop is a major theme:

All of you follow the bishop as Jesus Christ followed the Father, and the presbyters as you would the apostles; and revere the deacons as the command of God. Let no one do anything pertaining to the church apart from the bishop.
Let that Eucharist be considered valid which is that of the bishop or of someone authorized by him. Wherever the bishop appears, there let the people be, just as wherever Jesus Christ is, there is the Catholic Church. It is not proper to baptize or have an *agape* apart from the bishop. Whatever he approves is also pleasing to God. . . .
It is good to know God and the bishop. Whoever honors the bishop has been honored by God. Whoever does anything without the bishop's knowledge serves the devil.[22]

Similar injunctions are given to the young Polycarp, the bishop in Smyrna: "Vindicate your office with all diligence. . . . Keep unity in mind. . . . Let nothing be done without your approval. . . . Seek out every one by name."[23] After Ignatius, the threefold ministry of a single bishop, with his council of presbyters and assisting deacons, soon became universal in the churches.

The manner of ordination of these three orders of ministry is seldom noted in our early sources. It is generally assumed that ordination was by prayer with the laying on of hands, in accordance with Jewish custom for admission to the council of elders and to the rabbinate.[24] In the Book of Acts, the Twelve ordained the seven by prayer and laying on of hands (6:6)—an act which later came to be understood as the origin of the diaconate;[25] and at Antioch, prophets and teachers set apart Barnabas and Saul (Paul) by prayer and laying on of hands for their missionary tasks (13:2–3). The Pastoral Epistles reflect the same custom with regard to Timothy.[26] More often, however, the words for "appoint" are used, without any indication of the manner of induction into office.[27]

The ceremony of laying on of hands was not confined to commissioning and ordaining; it was used for blessings, healings, exorcisms, and impartings of the Spirit.[28] In each case it was the prayer or words used that defined the purpose of the ceremony. We have no extant prayers for ordination until the time of Hippolytus of Rome in the early third century. The bishop was ordained by other bishops in the presence of the congregation which had chosen him and had given its consent to his election. The prayer calls upon God:

Pour forth your princely Spirit whom you gave to your beloved Son Jesus Christ, and whom he gave to his holy apostles, who established the Church in every place as your sanctuary, for the unceasing glory and praise of your Name.

Father, you know the hearts of all: Grant to this your servant whom you have chosen for the episcopate, that he may feed your holy flock and serve you as your high priest without blame, ministering day and night to propitiate without ceasing your countenance and offer the holy gifts of your Church, and have power, by the Spirit of high priesthood, to remit sins according to your commandment, to ordain according to your precept, and so loose every bond according to the power you gave to the apostles. . . .[29]

A presbyter was ordained by the bishop with other presbyters who joined with him in the laying on of hands, with this prayer:

Grant him the Spirit of grace and counsel of the presbyterate, that he may sustain and govern your people with a pure heart, as you did look upon your chosen people and did command Moses that he should choose presbyters with that Spirit whom you gave to your servant Moses. . . .[30]

There is nothing said here of any priestly or liturgical functions of the presbyter—only his care and governance of the Church with the bishop and his fellow presbyters. When, then, did presbyters come to exercise a priestly office with or for the bishop?

It is well known that in the New Testament writings, priestly terms in a Christian sense—as opposed to Jewish and pagan uses—are applied to Christ only or to his Church as a whole. No Christian minister is ever called a priest.[31] In noncanonical writings of the late first and early second centuries, the use of priestly terms in contexts dealing with ministry and worship first appears, but is not developed. In First Clement, for example, the divine order of high priest, priests, and Levites, and their cultic service in the Old Testament, is employed as an example for the Corinthians not to transgress the "appointed rule" *(canon)* of due regard for each to observe his own rank in the liturgy. But no equivalence is made of these Old Testament ministries with those of the Church.[32] The *Didache* also refers to true prophets who settle in a community and receive their due offerings of firstfruits, for "they are your high priests."[33] The New Testament conception of the whole Church as a priesthood continued to be expressed, however, on into the third century.[34]

The first use of "priest" to denote a Christian minister occurs in the Western Church, and is employed only for a bishop. We have already seen this usage in the ordination prayer for a bishop by Hippolytus of Rome, who designates him as a "high priest." In one instance, Hippolytus claims the title for himself, as a successor of the apostles.[35] About the same time (A.D. 200), Tertullian in North Africa refers to the bishop as *summus sacerdos* ("high priest").[36] Neither writer is clear about any sacerdotal character to the presbyterate. From the evidence available to us, one could argue either way.

In Hippolytus' account of the ordination of a bishop, the new bishop celebrates the Eucharist after his consecration. When the deacons have presented to him the oblation, he lays his hands on it "with all the presbytery" and begins the great prayer of thanksgiving. This could be a concelebration with his presbyters, or it may refer simply to the fact that the presbyters stood about him as his honored counselors. It is clear that the bishop alone lays hands on the oblation and he alone says the prayer.[37] In another injunction, singular in early Christian literature, Hippolytus says that a confessor—one who was imprisoned and punished in persecution—was thereby given "the honor of the presbyterate" without the laying on of hands; but if he was appointed a bishop, he should receive the laying on of hands.[38]

Tertullian's other references to sacerdotal office or function occur in polemical contexts. During his years as a Catholic he inveighed against heretics, as having false "priesthoods and ministries";[39] and this included their permission for women to exercise them. Their lack of proper authority and discipline is summarized in the following famous invective:

In the first place, one cannot tell who is a catechumen and who is baptized [*fidelis*]. . . . Catechumens are initiated before they are instructed. As for the women of the heretics, how insolent they are!—they presume to teach, to argue, to perform exorcisms, to promise cures, perchance even to baptize. Their ordinations are thoughtless, capricious, and unstable. . . . So today one is a bishop, and tomorrow another; today one is a deacon, tomorrow a reader; today one is a presbyter, tomorrow a layman; for they also give laymen charge of sacerdotal functions.[40]

After Tertullian joined the charismatic sect of the Montanists, he turned his fire upon the Catholics—notably Bishop Agrippinus of Carthage, whom he sarcastically called a *pontifex maximus* and self-styled "Bishop of bishops," because of his lenient penance for those guilty of grievous sins. Only a Church led by spiritual men, such as apostles and prophets, said Tertullian, had such power, not a Church with "a number of bishops." For this right was "the Lord's, not the servant's; it was of God himself, not of the priest."[41]

Only toward the middle of the third century do we have precise indications of priestly office committed to presbyters. This was no doubt due to the increase of members in the larger churches, where the bishop could not always preside at every Eucharist; and, in the disruptive situation created by the general persecutions of the 250s, churches whose bishops had been martyred or had gone into hiding depended for their ministrations as well as their governance upon the presbyters.[42]

In the East, Origen at Caesarea in Palestine distinguishes in one place "those who preside over the people"—the bishops—from those from whom he might humbly receive counsel: namely, "an inferior priest, or even a layman or a pagan."[43] In the West, Bishop Cyprian of Carthage, in a communication to Bishop Stephen in Rome, refers to the readmission to the Catholic Church of presbyters and deacons, who in a schismatic church (namely, the Novations) had, as priests and ministers, offered false and sacrilegious sacrifices at the altar.[44] In connection with this same schism, Bishop Cornelius of Rome wrote a letter to his episcopal colleague in Antioch, in which he noted that the church in Rome had only one bishop, but also forty-six presbyters; seven deacons; seven subdeacons; forty-two acolytes; fifty-two exorcists, readers, and doorkeepers; and fifteen hundred widows and distressed persons on the rolls of Church support.[45]

In Alexandria the organization was singular. At first, the Bishop of Alexandria presided not only over the parishes or communities of the city, but over all church congregations in Egypt. He was chosen by the presbyters who presided over the parishes of the city from among their number; but the manner of his ordination is obscure.[46] During the third century, the Bishop of Alexandria provided bishops for several of the larger towns of Egypt; but many towns and villages remained in the charge of a presbyter.[47] This was contrary to the prevailing custom in other provinces of the Roman Empire, such as Syria, Asia Minor, Italy, and North Africa, where every town community had its bishop, even if there were only one congregation.

In such small towns the bishop continued to be the priest of all liturgical celebrations. A church order from Syria, dated variously within the third century, makes this clear. Its editor notes:

Presbyters are mentioned in the *Didascalia* only as it were by the way.... They are appointed by the bishop, and their characteristic function is to be the bishop's counsellors, or the council of the Church. In church they have their seats about the bishop's throne at the eastern end. Along with the deacons they assist the bishop in all cases of judgement which come before him. . . .

In a small church, such as the *Didascalia* appears to contemplate, in which public worship was regularly conducted by the bishop, the presbyters would find no independent role as preachers or celebrants, and as a mere *collegium* they would stand for the most part in the background. They had no administrative or pastoral work to bring them into prominence.[48]

NOTES

1. Similarly, the contraction appears in the Old Saxon *prēstar*, the Old French *prestre*, and the German *priester*.

2. The exception is the quasi-canonical letter of the Institution of Ministers, p. 569.

3. In rubrics, pp. 432, 434, 438, 439, and "Presbyterate," p. 420; in the text, p. 439.

4. Cf. Lk 15:25; Acts 2:17; 1 Tim 5:1–2; Tit 2:2–6; 1 Pet 5:5; 1 Clement 1:3, 3:3, 21:6; Pseudo-Barnabas, *Epistle* 13:5; Hermas, *Shepherd*, Vis. 3:1, 11, 12.

5. Cf. Mk 7:3–5 with Mt 15:2; Heb 11:2; 1 Clement 44:5; Irenaeus, *Against Heresies* 111.2 and (as quoted) in Eusebius, *Church History*, vol 24, 14–16.

6. Num 11:16 ff.; cf. Ex 24:1. See Roland de Vaux, *Ancient Israel: Its Life and Institutions* (New York: McGraw-Hill Book Co., 1965), Index under "Elders," p. 554.

7. Lk 22:66; Acts 22:5; of a Christian presbytery, 1 Tim 4:14. Ignatius of Antioch (ca. A.D. 115) compared Christian presbyters to a *synedrion:* "of the apostles," *Magnesians* 6:1, "of God," *Tralles* 3:1, "of the bishop," *Philadelphians* 8:1.

8. See "Sanhedrin," *The Mishnah,* trans. Herbert Danby (Oxford: Clarendon Press, 1933), pp. 382 ff. Cf. Mk 13:9 with Mt 10:17.

9. Ibid., "Megillah," pp. 201, 206.

10. George Foot Moore, *Judaism in the First Centuries of the Christian Era: The Age of the Tannaim,* vol. 1 (Cambridge, Mass: Harvard University Press, 1927), pp. 289 ff. At Rome each synagogue had its own council with officials called *archons.*

11. Acts 15:2, 4, 6; 22–23; 16:4; 21:18; cf. 11:30.

12. Acts 14:23; Tit 1:5.

13. 1 Thess 5:12; cf. Rom 12:8.

14. Acts 20:17 ff.; 1 Tim 5:17; Jas 5:14; 1 Pet 5:1–4; Hermas, *Shepherd*, vis. 2:4; 3.

15. The term "bishop" *(episcopos)* literally means "overseer." In Hellenistic associations the title was used for financial managers or treasurers. A synonymous title was that of "superintendent" *(epimeletes)*. The latter term was used by Josephus to denote the stewards or managers of the property and income of the Jewish communities of Essenes (*Wars of the Jews* ii. 8, 3; *Antiquities of the Jews* xviii. 1, 5). The Dead Sea Scrolls have revealed much more about the duties of this manager, called the *mebaqqer*. In addition to being a fiscal manager, he was the president of the community assembly, its teacher, master, and director of novices; and in one document was likened to a shepherd of his sheep (IQS 6:12–14; CD 13:7–9; in the first reference he is called also *paqid*, the usual Hebrew equivalent of *episcopos*). As a layman, however, he did not preside over the cultic assemblies of the community; this was in the charge of a priest. See Frank Moore Cross, Jr., *The Ancient Library of Qumran and Modern Biblical Studies* (Garden City: Doubleday and Co., 1958), pp. 175–176; Matthew Black, *The Scrolls and Christian Origins* (New York: Charles Scribner's Sons, 1961), pp. 115–117.

These analogies to the Christian bishop have often been remarked; but there is a difference. In all references to the Christian bishop, he has charge not only of the offerings of the people; he is also their liturgical president. In this, he functions more after the pattern of the ruler of the synagogue. See my article, "Bishop," *The Interpreter's Dictionary of the Bible*, vol.1. (New York-Nashville: Abingdon Press, 1962), pp. 441–443; Edwin Hatch, *The Organization of the Early Christian Churches*, 4th ed. (London: Longmans, Green and Co., 1892), chap 2; Martin Dibelius and Hans Conzelmann, *The Pastoral Epistles* "Hermeneia" (Philadelphia: Fortress Press, 1972), pp. 54–57.

16. It is possible to see these men as having the charisma of "governments" and "helps"; cf. 1 Cor 12:28 with 1 Cor 12:4–11; Rom 12:6–8.

17. 15:1–2. The date, provenance, and authority of the *Didache* is constantly debated. It is a "church order," with catechetical, liturgical, and ministerial regulations, that utilizes older sources. The single Greek manuscript extant probably dates from the second century and comes from Alexandria; cf. Cyril C. Richardson, ed., *Early Christian Fathers*, The Library of Christian Classics, vol. 1 (Philadelphia: Westminster Press, 1953), pp. 162–163.

18. We are not concerned here with the question of apostolic succession, or of who these "eminent men" were. They may have been apostolic delegates such as Timothy and Titus, notable prophets and teachers, or even presbyters.

19. 44:1–6.

20. *The Church and Its Organization in Primitive and Catholic Times* (London: Longmans, Green and Co., 1904), pp. 350 ff. The word "place" is often used to mean a position or office: Acts 1:25; 1 Clement 40:5; Ignatius, *Smyrnaeans* 6:1, *Polycarp* 1:2.

21. Acts 20:28; 1 Clement 44:6; 54:1–2. Cf. 1 Tim 3:1–13 with 5:17 ff.; Tit 1:5–9.

22. *Smyrnaeans* 8:1–9:1.

23. *Polycarp* 1:2; 4:1–2.

24. J. Newman, *Semikhah (Ordination): A Study of Its Origin, History and Function in Rabbinic Literature* (Manchester: Manchester University Press, 1950).

25. So interpreted first in Irenaeus, *Against Heresies*, i. 26, 3:iii. 12, 10; iv. 15, 1.

26. 1 Tim 4:14, by the presbytery; 2 Tim 1:5, by the apostle.

27. *Cheirotonein* in Acts 14:23; *Didache* 15:1; *kathistenai* in Tit 1:5; 1 Clement 42:4; 44:2–3. Only in the fourth century did *cheirotonein* become a synonym for "ordain"; a possible though problematic mid-third-century precedent in Eusebius *Church History* vi. 43, 10: Pseudo-Clement *Epistle to James* 2.

28. Cf. Mk 10:16 with Mt 19:13; Mk 8:23, 25; Acts 5:12 (cf. Mk 6:2); Acts 8:18; 9:17; 19:6; Heb 6:2.

29. *The Apostolic Tradition* 3, Dom B. Botte, ed., pp. 8–9.

30. Ibid., 7, pp. 20–21.

31. See my article, "Priests in the New Testament," *The Interpreter's Dictionary of the Bible,* vol 3 (New York-Nashville: Abingdon Press, 1962), pp. 889–891. In a recent careful analysis based on Jn 17 rather than the Epistle to the Hebrews, Andre Feuillet, *The Priesthood of Christ and His Ministers* (Garden City: Doubleday and Co., 1975) sees Christ's priesthood transmitted to his apostles and their successors; but the difference between bishops and presbyters is blurred.

32. 40–41, 43.

33. 13:3; cf. 15:1; note 17 above.

34. Justin Martyr, *Dialogue with Trypho* 116:3; Irenaeus, *Against Heresies* iv. 8, 3; Origen, *Commentary on John* i. 2.

35. *Refutation of All Heresies (Philosophumena)* i. pref. This passage is the principal basis for the tradition that Hippolytus was an antipope in Rome.

36. *On Baptism* 17.

37. *The Apostolic Tradition* 4, Botte, ed., pp. 10–11.

38. Ibid., 9, pp. 28–29.

39. *On the Prescription of Heretics* 29.

40. Ibid., 41. Since Gnostic heretics believed that the final resurrection had already taken place, there was no longer any distinction of the sexes (cf. Mt 22:30). For Tertullian's view of women as ministers, see also his *On the Veiling of Virgins* 9: "Women are not permitted to speak in the church, or to teach, baptize, offer [the Eucharist]; nor are they to claim any masculine function, much less any sacerdotal office."

41. *On Modesty* 1, 21. Some scholars believe Tertullian was attacking Bishop Callistus of Rome; for the literature, see Johannes Quasten, *Patrology,* vol. 2 (Westminster: The Newman Press, 1953), p. 313.

42. In Carthage, during the Decian persecution of 250–251 when Bishop Cyprian was in hiding, certain confessors and presbyters took it upon themselves even to usurp the bishop's prerogative of admitting lapsed Christians back into communion; see Cyprian *Letters* xiii-sv.

43. *Homilies on Exodus* xi. 6, delivered after A.D. 244. Since these homilies

are extant only in a late fourth-century translation, it is possible that the original Greek text has been revised.

44. *Letters* lxxii. 2.

45. Quoted in Eusebius, *Church History* vi. 43, 11. One detects here the origin of the later twenty-five titular or parish churches of Rome, each under two presbyters for ministration of the sacraments; and also the seven regions, each under a deacon assisted by a subdeacon.

46. See W. Telfer, "Episcopal Succession in Egypt," *The Journal of Ecclesiastical History*, III (1952), 1–13.

47. Athanasius, *Apology Against the Arians* 85; Jerome, *Letters* cxlvi. 1, 6. Cf. Hans Lietzmann, "The Founding of the Church Universal," *A History of the Early Church*, vol. 2 (New York: Charles Scribner's Sons, 1950), pp. 64–65.

48. R. Hugh Connolly, *Didascalia Apostolorum* (Oxford: Clarendon Press, 1929), pp. xxxix-xl. The most thorough survey of the Christian communities and bishoprics in the Roman Empire before the Council of Nicaea in 325 is that of Adolf Harnack, *The Expansion of Christianity in the First Three Centuries,* vol. 2 (New York: G. P. Putnam's Sons, 1905), pp. 240 ff.

chapter 9

THE IDEAL PARSON OF THE NEWLY REFORMED ENGLISH CHURCH

Frederica Harris Thompsett

In 1551 the new Bishop of Gloucester, John Hooper—a powerful preacher and zealous reformer eager to establish the reformed faith in his diocese—was at best dismayed when visitation records of his parish clergy indicated that out of 311 clergy, 168 were unable to repeat the Decalogue, 9 could not count the Commandments, and 33 were unable to locate them in Scripture; moreover, there were 10 clergy who could not repeat the Lord's Prayer, 9 who could not locate it in Scripture, and 34 who were unable to name its author. Such statistics might appear incredulous given today's general expectations that a clergyman be a trained, educated professional. However, throughout Christian history, models for ministry have evolved to suit the religious intentions of various cultures.[1] The chronological focus for this essay is on the early days of the English Reformation. In particular we will examine expectations for the parish clergyman in the reign of the Protestant Josiah, the child-king, Edward VI (1547–1553). In this hey day of religious reform and liturgical achievement (e.g. the Prayer Books of 1549 and 1552), increased attention was given to realigning and reinvigorating the functions and practice of parochial ministry. In this essay a number of questions will be raised concerning the process of changing expectations of ministry: not only what model for ministry was suggested by mid-Tudor reformers and how it was to be achieved, but also why Englishmen, among both the laity and the clergy, were convinced of the need to reform parish clergy.

Certainly there was room for improvement of the mid-Tudor clerical estate. Most of the parochial clergy (with the exception of clergy in

83

London and the university towns) were casually educated. They might
have attended a local ABC school, or one of the Latin grammar schools;
or a neighboring clergyman might have taught them to read. University
graduates, seeking more lucrative posts, were seldom resident in parochial livings. Few parsons received any specific training in theology,
and many were narrowly informed. They tended to focus on local
problems, to be comfortable with traditional practices of worship, and
to suspect innovation in general. Economically, the value of their livings varied considerably, as did the sources of income (tithes, fees,
farming, etc.). It has been estimated that three-quarters of the parochial
incomes were inadequate. Moreover, the parson's income, like that of
his parishioners, was threatened by inflation. Socially, many of the parochial clergy came from the class they served. Once a clergyman was
fortunate enough to find a benefice (often after years of low-paid service
as a stipendiary curate) his social base as parson of the village was
secure, though social expectations of his position might severely tax his
finances. Some parsons were also in need of assistsants to adequately
serve their parishes, but often they did not have the means to hire them.
In sum, parochial clergy in the early years of the Reformation were
ill-equipped by training, resources, or temperament to wean their
parishes away from the familiar patterns of worship, let alone attract
them to Protestantism.[2]

Anticlerical attitudes, particularly indignation and resentment of
greedy clerics, were familiar components of English medieval thought.
No doubt there were some greedy and immoral Tudor parsons (although anticlerical polemics tended to magnify such evidence), but
certainly the early Reformation clergy were not worse, spiritually, than
their medieval predecessors. Yet during the Reformation there was a
more constructive dimension to anticlerical thought which took the
form of an intensified concern for the provision of an adequate ministry.
The laity were in part responsible for this transformation as their expectations and standards for clerical performance perceptibly increased.
Many laymen seemed less willing to tolerate the conventional abuses
of pluralism, simony, and absenteeism. One central impetus for their
changing attitudes was that the invention of the printing press eventually led to a general diffusion of education. Many Englishmen struggled
to learn or improve their reading skills and many developed a pro-
nounced taste for religious literature. Hugh Latimer, a popular
preacher and experienced reformer, wryly noted in a 1549 sermon
before the Court that some of the laity were better learned in Scripture
than the clergy.[3] Although ignorance and superstition were by no
means arrested by accessibility to inexpensive books, standards of lay
education were increasing and some laymen began to set a higher
premium on an educated parochial clergy.

The impetus for reform of the clergy was further enhanced by the unrelenting social and economic challenges to mid-Tudor society. A long inflationary spiral, unstable patterns of landholding, repeated debasements in the value of the coinage, expensive military campaigns, rebellions among the common people in the summer of 1549, plus the insecurity of a period of minority rule—these tensions propelled contemporary criticism and debate. Accordingly, as there was little distinction in Tudor thought between secular and spiritual issues, many of these complaints were quickly absorbed into religious controversy where they served to refuel anticlerical diatribes. The new enemy was envisioned as an even heartier brand of "Protestant" greed. Contemporary critics argued that popish monks and priests had been replaced by extortioners who fed off the spoils of the Reformation. They pointed to the social and economic ills of society as evidence that the Church's mission was failing. Individual members of the laity were more reluctant, given the rise in prices, to pay even traditional fees to clergy. Some argued that they wanted better value for their money from their parsons.[4] Anticlerical attitudes were exacerbated by social and economic dislocation and there was a heightened demand for reform.

The former model of ministry, suited to a culture in which religion was a ritual method of living, was also proving less viable. Under the prolonged impact of the Reformation, functions of ministry, as practiced by the medieval parson, were becoming less distinct. According to an historian of religion and magic:

Protestantism thus presented itself as a deliberate attempt to take the magical elements out of religion, to eliminate the idea that rituals of the Church had about them a mechanical efficacy, and to abandon the effort to endow physical objects with supernatural qualities by special formulae of consecration. . . . The reformers set out to eliminate theatricality from church ritual and decoration, and to depreciate the status of the priesthood.[5]

Only a few theologically informed members of a parish might notice the lack of emphasis on the sacrificial character of the priesthood in the 1549 and 1552 Prayer Books, but most parishioners paid attention only to changes within their local church—removing the rood screen, defacing images of saints, replacing the altar with a table, etc. Before their eyes much of the luster was withdrawn from the drama of worship and thereby from the principal actors. When, early in Edward VI's reign, clergy were officially permitted to marry, yet another barrier that set the parson apart from the laity was removed. The clerical office itself was suffering a loss of distinction.

The central reason why there was concern for providing skilled ministry was that a well-trained clergy could help meet the polemical needs of competing professions of faith. It was abundantly clear to Bishop Hooper, even before his diocesan visitation, and to other English clerics and statesmen engaged in laying the foundations of Protestantism, that reform of the parochial clergy was more than a familiar religious ideal, it was a matter of necessity. The fate of alterations in religious policy engraved in statutes, liturgies, and injunctions, rested on the parish clergy of rural England. If these changes were to be maintained, and the reformed faith was to prosper, then the parochial base must be firm. English reformers also realized that traditional functions of ministry must be realigned to suit the reformed Church. In sermons and other polemical tracts, reformers resolutely began to discuss and define ministerial functions that were in harmony with the intentions of Protestantism.

Attention focused on preaching. English reformers of the 1530s, 40s and early 50s concurred in defining ministry as exhortation of the word of God. In his colorful sermons Hugh Latimer insisted that salvation was a preaching and not a "massing" matter, and that preaching was necessary for a spiritually starving people because it was "meat" not "strawberries."[6] In a more complicated analogy Thomas Becon—a prolific preacher and homilist—described the preacher as the "eye" who allows the "light" of Scripture to enliven the "body" of the congregation. Becon added that if a parson could not preach, this was evidence that he was sent by the devil, not by Christ.[7] Other traditional functions of ministry extended from the preaching base, as in Becon's 1550 description of the ideal pastor:

The spiritual minister is appointed of God to rule with "the sword of the Spirit, which is the word of God," to rebuke sinners with the law, yea, and to excommunicate them if they be obstinate and will not repent, to comfort and cherish the weak with the sweet promises of the holy scripture, to encourage the strong, and to exhort them forward until they wax ancient, and be perfect in Christ's religion, to minister the sacraments, to make collections for the poor, to maintain hospitality for the relief of the needy.[8]

There was also repeated insistence that the parson lead an exemplary life, mirroring Christian virtues in his actions and words. If this was not done, more than one layman noted, the doctrines preached by the parson would have no credence. In England, as on the continent, reformed notions of ministry were emphatically grounded on proclamation of the word.

Henrician and Edwardian reformers maintained that in addition to establishing the true faith in England, preaching ministers would contain sedition and promote social harmony. Well-trained preachers could convince their parishioners, whether beggars or commoners, to remain content within their vocations. In fact a few reformers, who in 1549 were anxious to absolve themselves from any connection with social agitation, noted that one of the causes of the recent rebellions was the lack of good preaching, and they threatened that brutality might continue if able preachers were not provided.[9] They extended their arguments to suggest that preaching parsons could become the linchpins of social harmony by awakening parishioners to the dangers of oppression within society and encouraging charity and stewardship to the poor. Robert Crowley, a Tudor pamphleteer who was remarkably sensitive to the plight of the poor, envisioned the ideal parson as a custodian of the social, as well as the spiritual, welfare of his communicants. Throughout their discussions of need for preaching clergymen, the reformers were persuaded that the English Church would be invigorated when its ministers learned to deal directly with the central issues of their society.

To achieve their objective of a preacher in every parish, the reformers advocated sending aspiring ministers to the universities, and then providing parsons with decent livings. The first provision was problematical for two reasons. The reformers had to insist—to counter those who suggested that a good preacher was the handiwork of God and not of man—that while men should trust in divine inspiration, they should not presume upon or tempt God.[10] Hugh Latimer and Thomas Lever, a young preacher who was particularly sensitive to the need for training parochial clergy, were also worried about the decay of universities and other schools and the dearth of divinity students. Latimer noted that there were 10,000 fewer students than twenty years earlier, and that unless immediate attention was given to reviving schools and universities, there would be very little divinity in England.[11] He and Lever urged that schools and scholars should be supported by generous charitable giving. Lever addressed the need for adequate livings in an ingenious sermon on Christ's feeding of the five thousand. He implored the king to gather together all benefices and other spiritual offices and fees (which had supported only a privileged few) and then to redistribute them to honest preachers, thereby feeding the multitude. His plea was: "For the love of God give your servants wages."[12] Bishop Hooper, with customary zeal for the welfare of the laity, noted that the maintenance of an educated, well-paid parish clergy would eventually lead to a better educated, less superstitious laity. The reformers' hope was that by reviving educational opportunities for clergy and by paying parsons well, the new religion could be zealously and ably promoted.

Further local and regional research on the impact of Reformation policies is needed before we can estimate whether the reformers' ambitions were realized. Various local studies of the village parson in Queen Elizabeth's reign (1559–1603), suggest that the standard of living and of education (judging by the larger libraries of the late Elizabethan parson) had improved. But the model of the ideal parish clergyman advocated by Henrician and Edwardian reformers did not have enough time to be implemented. Advancement of Protestant policies came to an abrupt halt with the death of the king in 1553 and the reversion to Roman Catholicism under Mary Tudor (1553–1559).

England's evolution toward Protestantism was a long and complex process. Historians may have underestimated the difficulties of effecting Reformation policies at the local level. Even Bishop Hooper, with all his haste for founding the reformed Church in Gloucester, had to combat ignorance (in itself a conservative force) among the clergy and laity. Religious indifference too was an enemy of reform. Latimer frankly acknowledged that there were lots of people who preferred to hear stories of Robin Hood rather than a sermon. One parson ingeniously saved money on books, and avoided changing services, by simply crossing out references to King Edward in his copy of the 1552 Prayer Book and substituting Queen Mary's name.[13] Presumably he used this Prayer Book during Mary's reign. Many rural parochial clergy were neither hot nor cold, nor perhaps even exposed to Reformation policies and ideals.

Latimer, Hooper, Lever, Becon, and a number of other inspired preachers and reformers were in part responsible for laying the foundations of English Protestantism in Edward VI's reign. Their repeated public advocacy of the need for preaching parsons may not have been appreciated by most of the mid-Tudor parochial clergy, but their exhortations did not fall entirely on deaf ears. Bishop Hooper, as we have seen, had reason to despair over his parish clergy, but he had great confidence in the laity of his diocese. Hooper was hopeful that the laity would expect and eventually demand well-educated, preaching parsons. He thanked God:

For that he hath mercifully inclined the hearts of the people to wish and hunger for the word of God as they do. . . . there lacketh nothing among the people but sober, learned and wise men.[14]

NOTES

1. Urban T. Holmes, III, *The Future Shape of Ministry* (New York: The Seabury Press, 1971); see especially Part 1, "The Evolving Function of Ministry."

2. Two recent books proved particularly helpful to this discussion of the

Tudor parish clergy: Peter Heath, *The English Parish Clergy on the Eve of the Reformation* (London: Routledge & Kegan Paul, 1969); and Christopher Haigh, *Reformation and Resistance in Tudor Lancashire* (Cambridge: At the University Press, 1975). One of the most useful surveys of the Reformation in England is A. G. Dickens, *The English Reformation* (New York: Schocken Books, 1964).

3. Hugh Latimer, *The Works of Hugh Latimer*, ed. G. E. Corrie for the Parker Society, 2 vols. (Cambridge: At the University Press, 1844–45), I. 122. The spelling and punctuation in all sixteenth-century quotations has been modernized. On the popular appetite for religious literature, see H. S. Bennett, *English Books and Readers, 1457–1557* (Cambridge: At the University Press, 1952).

4. *A Discourse of the Common Weal of this Realm of England (1549)*, ed. E. Lamond (Cambridge: At the University Press, 1893), p. 134. This text is now thought to have been written by the Tudor statesman, Thomas Smith.

5. Keith Thomas, *Religion and the Decline of Magic: Studies in Popular Beliefs in Sixteenth- and Seventeenth-Century England* (London: Weidenfeld & Nicholson, 1971), p. 87.

6. Latimer, *Works*, I, 178 & 62. Latimer's justly famous "Sermon on the Plough" (1548) is well worth reading as an example of Tudor homiletics; ibid., pp. 59–78.

7. Thomas Becon, *Works*, ed. J. Ayre for the Parker Society, 2 vols. (Cambridge: At the University Press, 1843–44), II, 421 & 320.

8. Ibid., p. 616. A similar description of a minister was stated in 1550 by Thomas Lever, *Sermons*, ed. E. Arber (London: n.p., 1871), p. 74.

9. Latimer, *Works*, I, 269; and Becon, *Works*, II, 595–96.

10. Latimer, *Works*, I, 269. The same issue was discussed by the Christian humanist, Thomas Starkey, in *A Dialogue between Cardinal Pole and Thomas Lupset* (1538), ed. K. M. Burton (London: Chatto & Windus, 1948), p. 187.

11. Ibid. A recent analysis of Tudor education suggests that Latimer may have overestimated the decline in university students; Joan Simon, *Education and Society in Tudor England* (Cambridge: At the University Press, 1966), pp. 220, 248.

12. Lever, *Sermons*, p. 74. Lever delivered his sermon on feeding the multitude in 1550; ibid., pp. 53–90.

13. *The Boke of Common Praier, and Administracion of the Sacramentes, and Other Rites and Ceremonies in the Churche of England* (London: Richard Grafton, 1552). This extremely rare copy of the 1552 Prayer Book is in the library of Seabury-Western Theological Seminary. There are other interesting alterations in the text including crossing out the phrase in the Litany which asks for deliverance "from the tyranny of the Bishop of Rome, and all his detestable enormities," ibid., sig. B iiii.

14. This quote is from a letter written by Hooper in 1552 and is cited in an informative article by F. Douglas Price, "Gloucester Diocese under Bishop Hooper," *Transactions of the Bristol and Gloucestershire Archaeological Society*, LX (1939). p. 112.

chapter 10

THE MEANING OF ORDAINED PRIESTHOOD IN ECUMENICAL DIALOGUES

Herbert J. Ryan

In contemporary theology there is no question more difficult, more controversial or more urgent than the meaning of the ordained ministry. The difficulty arises not only from the pastoral aspects of the question but from the different decisions that the Christian churches have made in the course of history to assure that in differing cultural and political circumstances the life of the Gospel be lived meaningfully, Christ's message preached intelligibly and the saving mission which Christ received from the Father and entrusted to his Apostles be carried out faithfully in the Spirit. The neuralgic question which underlies the meaning of the ordained ministry is that of the apostolicity of the Church. Apostolicity is the technical theological term that grapples with the whole cluster of problems related to the question of how a Christian community may know that its life and message are authentically in continuity with the early churches formed by Jesus' disciples to carry on Christ's saving mission.[1]

The meaning of the ordained ministry is most certainly controversial. Each Christian church maintains that it is in living continuity with the early Church and that its witness of sacramental life and preaching makes the person and message of Christ meaningful for today's world. Yet not all Christian churches are in agreement concerning the most obvious questions about the ordained ministry. The first two world conferences on Faith and Order held at Lausanne in 1927 and Edinburgh in 1937 recognized the need for a "ministry acknowledged in every part of the Church as possessing the sanction of the whole Church."[2] Such a situation still does not exist. Yet if one may boldly summarize fifty years of ecumenical dialogue on the ordained ministry it would appear that an ecumenical consensus is emerging which would propose that the nature and meaning of the ordained ministry in the whole Christian Church should conform in broad outline to the structure and understanding of the ordained ministry as it existed in the Church at the time of the first four Ecumenical Councils.

As an acknowledged historical leader in the world-wide ecumenical movement, the Episcopal Church has made an outstanding contribution to this emerging consensus. Yet the Episcopal Church, in keeping with the Anglican theological tradition, has not articulated a confessional statement on the nature of the ordained ministry.[3] As Anglicanism generally, so the Episcopal Church has consistently proposed that her doctrine and practice is that found in Scripture and taught by the Ecumenical Councils of the undivided Church. From this self-understanding the Episcopal Church has engaged in ecumenical dialogue on the nature of the ordained ministry. The agreed statements, study documents and proposals which have been the fruit of this dialogue do not represent an articulation of a confessional position. What they do represent are informed prudential judgments which officially appointed members of the Episcopal Church deem to be consistent with their Church's self-understanding of her doctrine and practice.

What are these ecumenical statements and what do they say about priesthood? In the last five years four ecumenical documents have been produced by groups with official representation from the Episcopal Church. They are: (1) in 1970 *A Plan of Union for the Church of Christ Uniting*,[4] (2) in 1972 *Lutheran-Episcopal Dialogue: A Progress Report*,[5] (3) in 1973 *Ministry and Ordination: A Statement on the Doctrine of the Ministry Agreed by the Anglican Roman Catholic International Commission* (Canterbury Statement),[6] (4) in 1975 *One Baptism, One Eucharist and a Mutually Recognized Ministry: Study Documents from the Faith and Order Commission of the World Council of Churches*.[7] Three of these ecumenical statements are entire books. The length of all four of them prevents their being quoted extensively. They ought really to be studied in full. Yet certain highlights from the statements and a brief comment may at least serve to acknowledge the great effort of ecumenical theology that they represent.

A Plan of Union of the Church of Christ Uniting contains an entire chapter on the ordained ministry of presbyters (priests), bishops and deacons which situates this ministry within the one ministry given by Christ to the Church.

The Section on the Ministry of Presbyters follows that on the Meaning of Ordination and the Care of the Ordained Ministers. This section gives a brief account of the meaning of presbyterate (priesthood) and then describes eight Functions and Responsibilities of Presbyters. Presbyters are (1) Preachers of the Word, (2) Celebrants of the Sacraments, (3) Teachers of the Gospel, (4) Leaders in Mission, (5) Prophets for God, (6) Pastoral Overseers and Administrators, (7) Ecumenical Leaders, (8) Participants in Discipline.

The Ministry of Presbyters

42   Presbyters, otherwise known as pastors, priests, or elders, called by God and authorized by the church, are ordained as ministers of the Word and sacraments, of the discipline of the church, and as teachers of the faith. From the beginning, the presbyterate of the church has shared and expressed in particular ways the ministry of Christ, who is redeemer, Lord, prophet, shepherd, teacher, high priest, intercessor, guardian, preacher, servant, and master. The ministry of the presbyter should reflect his call by Christ and his recognition by the people of God.

43   There have been in history many interpretations of the presbyterate and of its relationship with other ordained offices. The united church welcomes the diversity of these interpretations, but seeks to encourage new insights and understanding. All those who are recognized as ordained ministers in any one of the uniting churches at the time of unification will be recognized as ordained ministers by the uniting church. Prior to unification each ordained minister will choose whether to be a presbyter or a lay person in the united church. A lay elder who has been ordained to celebrate the Lord's Supper, or a ruling elder in any of the uniting churches, through the service of inauguration may become a presbyter in the united church. He may, however, choose to become a deacon or a layman.

"To Be Ministers of Christ," the seventh chapter of the *Plan of Union* is a rich statement on the meaning of the ordained priesthood. However, the chapter adopts a functional approach to ordained priesthood with the intention of being inclusive rather than precise. If one were to inquire how the ordained ministerial priesthood differs from the priesthood of all the baptised the answer would be that the priest is "ordained" and the baptised lay person is not. This functional answer points to a very serious weakness in the chapter. The chapter does not provide an adequate understanding of what sacramental ordination is. Ordination is rightly said to be "an act of the whole church." But is the "church" in this statement the local church or congregation with bishop, presbyters and laity or the universal (catholic) church? Who is the effective sacramental agent of the Holy Spirit in the act of ordination? Is it the bishop alone, the bishop joined with his presbyters or the laity joined with their presbyters and bishop? This question is passed over and points to the unresolved tension which runs throughout the chapter: the often brilliant juxtaposition of episcopal order and congregational polity.[8]

The Lutheran-Episcopal Dialogue did not explicitly deal with the question of the meaning of the presbyterate (priesthood). However, when treating the problem of apostolicity the dialogue necessarily touched on the ordained ministry. Its *Progress Report* provides an invaluable context for the understanding of the ordained priesthood. The text cited is from the joint report on Apostolicity that was produced at the fourth meeting of the dialogue at Minneapolis in April, 1971.

We agree that apostolicity belongs to the reality of the one holy catholic church; apostolicity is manifested in various ways in all areas of the church's life, and is guarded especially by common confession and through that function of the church designated as *episcope* (oversight).

We agree that this substance of apostolic succession must take different forms in differing places and times, if the Gospel is indeed to be heard and received. At the time of the Reformation, one of our communions in its place experienced the continuity of the episcopally ordered ministry as an important means of the succession of the Gospel; in various ways the other in its place was able to take its responsibility of the succession of the Gospel only by a new ordering of its ministry. We agree that by each decision the apostolicity of the ministry in question was preserved, and that each of our communions can and should affirm the decision of the other. Until the Lord of the church grants a new ordering of the church, each communion should respect the right of the other to honor the distinct history which mediates its apostolicity, and to continue that ordering of its ministry which its history has made possible. Within the one church, both the Anglican continuity of the episcopal order, and the Lutheran concentration on doctrine, have been means of preserving the apostolicity of the one church.

For the future, we agree that if either communion should be able to receive the gift of the other's particular apostolicity, without unfaithfulness to its own, the future of the church would surely be served. In any future ordering of the one church, there will be a ministry and within that ministry an *episcope*. The functional reality of *episcope* is in flux in both our communions. If we are faithful, we will *together* discover the forms demanded by the church's new opportunities, so that the church may have an *episcope* which will be an *episcope* of the apostolic Gospel. Similarly, any future unity of the church will be a unity of common confession. The functional reality of the common confessions of the past (their contemporary interpretation and use) is in flux in both our communions. Our faithfulness will be that we think and pray together seeking to be ready for a new common confession when the Lord shall give us the apostolic boldness to proclaim the Gospel with the freshness and vigor of our fathers in the faith.

The *Lutheran-Episcopal Dialogue* in fact has not directly treated the meaning of priesthood. It has, however, investigated the meaning of the ordained ministry and its role in the apostolicity of the Church. By so doing it has provided a theological context for a future detailed agreement on the nature of the ordained priesthood and how it differs from the priesthood of all believers. The *Lutheran-Episcopal Dialogue* situates the meaning of the ordained ministry, priesthood included, within the notion of *episcope* (oversight). *Episcope* is a God-given range of gifts which enable for service (*ministerium,* ministry) that only the ordained can perform.

Ministry and Ordination, the 1973 Canterbury Statement of ARCIC, deals directly with the question of priesthood. The similarities to both the *Plan of Union* and the *Lutheran-Episcopal Dialogue* are striking. By dealing directly with the question of ordination the Canterbury Statement clarifies a possible major ambiguity in the treatment afforded that question in the *Plan of Union.* By specifying what type of *episcope* only bishops and priests have, the Canterbury Statement expands on some of the same insights that the *Lutheran-Episcopal Dialogue* has expressed.

14. Ordination denotes entry into this apostolic and God-given ministry, which serves and signifies the unity of the local churches in themselves and with one another. Every individual act of ordination is therefore an expression of the continuing apostolicity and catholicity of the whole Church. Just as the original apostles did not choose themselves but were chosen and commissioned by Jesus, so those who are ordained are called by Christ in the Church and through the Church. Not only is their vocation from Christ but their qualification for exercising such a ministry is the gift of the Spirit: "our sufficiency is from God, who has qualified us to be ministers of a new covenant, not in a written code but in the Spirit" (2 Cor. 3:5–6). This is expressed in ordination, when the bishop prays God to grant the gift of the Holy Spirit and lays hands on the candidate as the outward sign of the gifts bestowed. Because ministry is in and for the community and because ordination is an act in which the whole Church of God is involved, this prayer and laying on of hands takes place within the context of the eucharist.

15. In this sacramental act,[c] the gift of God is bestowed upon the ministers, with the promise of divine grace for their work and for their sanctification; the ministry of Christ is presented to them as a model for their own; and the Spirit seals those whom he has chosen and consecrated. Just as Christ has united the Church inseparably with himself, and as God calls all the faithful to life-long discipleship, so the gifts and calling of God to the ministers are irrevocable. For this reason, ordination is unrepeatable in both our churches.

16. Both presbyters and deacons are ordained by the bishop. In the ordination

[c]Anglican use of the word 'sacrament' with reference to ordination is limited by the distinction drawn in the Thirty-nine Articles (Article XXV) between the two 'sacraments of the Gospel' and the 'five commonly called sacraments.' Article XXV does not deny these latter the name 'sacrament,' but differentiates between them and the 'two sacraments ordained by Christ' described in the catechism as 'necessary to salvation' for all men.

of a presbyter the presbyters present join the bishop in the laying on of hands, thus signifying the shared nature of the commission entrusted to them. In the ordination of a new bishop, other bishops lay hands on him, as they request the gift of the Spirit for his ministry and receive him into their ministerial fellowship. Because they are entrusted with the oversight of other churches, this participation in his ordination signifies that this new bishop and his church are within the communion of churches. Moreover, because they are representative of their churches in fidelity to the teaching and mission of the apostles and are members of the episcopal college, their participation also ensures the historical continuity of this church with the apostolic church and of its bishop with the original apostolic ministry. The communion of the churches in mission, faith and holiness, through time and space, is thus symbolized and maintained in the bishop. Here are comprised the essential features of what is meant in our two traditions by ordination in the apostolic succession.

The Canterbury Statement clarifies how the ordained priesthood differs from the priesthood of all believers by showing what ordination means. In ordination the person ordained receives the gift of *episcope* from the Holy Spirit. This gift, *episcope*, belongs "to another realm of the gifts of the Spirit" than those gifts received from the Holy Spirit at Baptism. At their ordination priests (and bishops) receive from the Holy Spirit a gift of liturgical *episcope* which enables them to preside at the eucharistic liturgy. The effective agent of the Holy Spirit in the act of ordaining a presbyter is the bishop joined with his presbyters. Through his membership in the college of bishops the ordaining bishop simultaneously represents the universal Church to his local church and his local church to the universal Church. The presbyters who join with the ordaining bishop in the laying on of hands represent their individual congregations to the local church. In this way presbyteral ordination is an act of the whole (catholic) Church. The Canterbury Statement explicitly relates how the ordination of a bishop is an act of the whole (catholic) Church and how the bestowal of *episcope* involves the notion of apostolicity in faith and ministry.

The most detailed ecumenical assessment of the meaning of the ordained ministry is the 1975 Faith and Order Commission Report, *One Baptism, One Eucharist and a Mutually Recognized Ministry.* The third section of this report is entitled simply "The Ministry." Excerpts from this section will provide a summary and conclusion to this brief article on the meaning of the ordained priesthood as it is expressed in ecumenical dialogue. The theology of the ordained priesthood which is emerging from these dialogues relates four key theological areas as aids to understanding what ordained priesthood means. These areas are: (1) apostolicity, (2) *episcope* (oversight), (3) ordination, (4) the difference between the ordained priesthood and the priesthood of all the baptised.

In the Faith and Order Report the ordained ministry is called the "special ministry." The report shows the connection between the "special ministry" and apostolicity.

13. In order that his redemptive work might be proclaimed and attested to the ends of the earth, and that its fruits might be communicated to man, Christ chose apostles and committed to them the word of reconciliation.[2] Within the first Christian communities the apostles exercised a unique and fundamental function, which could not be handed on. However, in so far as they bore special (but not exclusive) responsibility for proclaiming the message of reconciliation, establishing churches and building them up in the apostolic faith, their ministry had to be continued. Although there was a variety of gifts in the Early Church, the New Testament reports a setting apart to special ministry, distinctions of service were made.[3] *This special ministry* was essential then—it is essential in all times and circumstances. Such a ministry is exercised by persons who are called within the community and given gifts and authority to transmit the living testimony of the apostles.

The report defines the "special ministry" in terms of *episcope*.

15. *The essential and specific function of the special ministry is:* to assemble and build up the Christian community, by proclaiming and teaching the Word of God, and presiding over the liturgical and sacramental life of the eucharistic community. The Christian community and the special ministry are related to one another. The minister cannot exist and fulfil his task in isolation. He needs the support and encouragement of the community. On the other hand, the Christian community needs the special ministry which serves to coordinate and unite the different gifts in the community and to strengthen and enable the ministry of the whole People of God. But above all, this relationship and mutual dependence manifests that the Church is not master of the Word and Sacrament, nor the source of its faith, hope and unity. Christian life as well as the ministry are received from the living Christ in the Church.

Entrance into the "special ministry" is by ordination.

16. The setting apart by God for this special ministry requires from the side of the Church a recognition of which a form is already found in Apostolic times (for example, II Timothy 1:6f.) and which later became commonly known as ordination.

The meaning of ordination is initially and briefly described when the Report describes the limits upon the ordained person in the exercise of *episcope*.

18. The exercise of such ministry has authority which ultimately belongs to Christ who has received it from the Father (Matt. 28:18); it is in this sense a divine authority. On the other hand, since ordination is essentially a setting

apart with prayer for the gifts of the Holy Spirit for the continuing constitution and edification of the body, the authority of the ordained ministry is not to be understood as an individual possession of the ordained person but belongs to the whole community in and for which the minister is ordained. Authority in the name of God in its exercise must involve the participation of the whole community. The ordained minister manifests and exercises the authority of Christ in the way Christ himself revealed God's authority to the world: *in and through communion.*

The report then discusses ministry and priesthood.

20. Even if the New Testament never uses the terms "priest-hiereus" or "priesthood-hierateuma" to designate the ordained minister or the ministry, tradition has not been afraid of this usage. Although churches emerging from the Reformation avoid the word priesthood to designate the ordained ministry, churches of the catholic tradition employ this word in diverse forms: priestly ministry, ministerial priesthood, or, more recently, ministry of priesthood. The search for a reconciliation in ministries makes it especially useful to discuss this question of terms.

21. This manner of expression always refers the function of the priests to a priestly reality upon which theirs is based, but which exceeds it—that is, the unique priesthood of Christ and the royal and prophetic, common and universal priesthood of the baptized (I Peter 2:9; Rev. 1:6, 3:10, 20:6). The priesthood of Christ and the priesthood of the baptized community is a function of sacrifice and intercession. As Christ offers himself for all men, the Christian offers his whole being "as a living sacrifice" (Rom. 12:1). As Christ intercedes to the Father for all men, the Christian prays for the liberation of his human brothers. The minister, who participates, as every Christian does, in the priesthood of Christ, and of all the People of God, fulfils his particular priestly service in strengthening, building up and expressing the royal and prophetic priesthood of the faithful through the service of the Gospel, the leading of the liturgical and sacramental life of the eucharistic community, and intercession.

22. The ordained ministry is then of a completely new and different nature in relation to the sacrificial priesthood of the Old Testament. As He offers his life for the service of the mission in the world and of the edification of the Church, the minister is, as St. Paul says about himself, "a minister of Jesus Christ to the Gentiles in the priestly service of the gospel of God, so that the offering of the Gentiles may be acceptable, sanctified by the Holy Spirit" (Rom. 15:16).[9]

NOTES

1. An excellent treatment of apostolicity is "Catholicity and Apostolicity: Report of the Joint Working Group between the Roman Catholic Church and the World Council of Churches" in *Faith and Order: Louvain 1971.* World Council of Churches, Geneva, 1971, 133–158. The research papers that formed the basis for this report are published in *One in Christ* VI-3 (1970), 243–451.

2. T. Tatlow, "The World Conference on Faith and Order" in R. Rouse and S.C. Neill, *A History of the Ecumenical Movement 1517–1948.* The Westminster Press, Philadelphia, 1968, 405–441.

3. However the Episcopal Church does hold a position on the ordained ministry. Cf. "Statement of Faith and Order" (from the report of the Joint Commission on Approaches to Unity to the General Convention of 1949), Section D. *Documents on Church Unity.* The Seabury Press, Greenwich, 1962, 14–18. *Ibid.*, Section D, No. 3 treats the priesthood and diaconate. The Tenth Lambeth Conference dealt extensively with the question of the ordained ministry. Cf. *The Lambeth Conference 1968: Resolutions and Reports.* S.P.C.K. and Seabury Press, London and New York, 1968, 98–110. There is a good treatment of the ordained priesthood in *Ibid.*, 100–102. For the issues involved in this Conference and the nature of its documents cf. Herbert J. Ryan, S.J., "Lambeth '68: A Roman Catholic Theological Reflection," *Theological Studies* XXIX-4 (December, 1968), 597–636.

4. *A Plan of Union for the Church of Christ Uniting.* COCU, Princeton, 1970, 1–104.

5. *Lutheran-Episcopal Dialogue: A Progress Report.* Forward Movement Publications, Cincinnati, 1973, 1–175.

6. *Ministry and Ordination: A Statement on the Doctrine of the Ministry Agreed by the Anglican Roman Catholic International Commission* (Canterbury Statement), *Worship* XLVIII-I (January, 1974), 2–10.

7. *One Baptism, One Eucharist and a Mutually Recognized Ministry.* Faith and Order Commission of the Council of Churches, Geneva, 1975, 1–61.

8. For further perspectives on the *Plan of Union,* cf. *A Sense of Waiting: A Notebook of Resources and Background for a Study of a Plan of Union for the Church of Christ Uniting.* Ecumenical Office of the Episcopal Church, New York, 1972 and *COCU: A Catholic Perspective.* United States Catholic Conference, Washington, D.C. 1970, 1–48.

9. *Ibid.*, 34–35, nos. 20–22. The statement bears a close relation to Canterbury Statement no. 13. The Faith and Order Statement would have gained considerably in clarity here by showing that liturgical eucharistic *episcope* is what is meant by ordained priesthood. The ordained priesthood is different from the unique priesthood of Christ and from the priesthood of all the baptised. The statement attempts to relate these three priesthoods to one another without previously distinguishing them. This causes confusion in the statement. The clearest treatment of these three priesthoods is J.M.R. Tillard, *What Priesthood Has the Ministry.* Grove Press, Bramcote, Notts., 1973, 1–28.

PART III

Priestly Functions

chapter 11

THE PRIEST AND THE EUCHARIST

Louis Bouyer

The priest is, above all, the man responsible for the Eucharist. To see this as the most central of his functions is the best way to perceive the various aspects of his role in their proper perspective and organic unity. But this requires that we recover the full and wide vision of the Eucharist, or more precisely of the complete eucharistic celebration.

If it is true that the priest, as the minister par excellence of Christ, is to be a "man for others," it is in the full eucharistic celebration that "the others" are brought together, and reconciled to one another by being reconciled to God in Christ. Not only is the eucharistic celebration the supreme manifestation of this unique society, the Church of Christ, at once interpersonal and universal; it is also in and through this celebration itself that the Church, as St. Paul says, is "edified"; that is, is "built" out of "living stones" into that total body of Christ which is to become the temple of the Spirit. This building of the eucharistic temple in which we ourselves are introduced as so many living stones, implies the taking up of all our human activities into a higher reality. It involves not only the fulfillment of the ideal human society, the City of God among men, but the ultimate completion of the cosmos itself, so as to make God in Christ, through the Church, all in all things.

If we adopt this perspective, which is that of the New Testament, especially of the Epistle to the Ephesians, we have the most precise, and also the most inspiring and exalted vision of the total humanity and reality of the role of the priest.

Primarily—and I insist on this—because the eucharistic celebration is the Church seen in the making, and because the priest is, first of all, the minister of it, he is not a "man for others" in any vague or shallow meaning. He is the man who is to enable his fellow men to become fully themselves by living in the common fulfillment of the society of divine love among men, working together and individually to bring the world at large to its final goal, its own proper consummation.

The priest, in spite of the singularity of his vocation, is not an isolated man. He is to live among all sorts and conditions of men to help them to live together. He is to make them realize that their distinctive activities, their distinctive types of life are consonant and concordant parts of a great enthusiastic purpose within a most intimate but widely open community. They do not simply receive this community ready-made, but build it up—edify it—by their own unique and irreplaceable contributions into its ultimate perfection in Christ.

In this work the priest is to be the confidant of all, able not only to sympathize equally with all but to bring to all—in spite of his own limitations, inadequacies, and even shortcomings—what they need to find their place in the world and to be fully themselves, by being taken up into the most wonderful exchange, not only among all men, all created beings, but between the whole creation and its Creator—and everyone with his most personal Savior.

How can this be? We shall begin to discover it by considering in depth the first role the priest assumes in the celebration of the Eucharist, the ministry of the word of God to man. This is above all the ministry of the Gospel, the Good News of salvation in Christ.

This ministry of the word, which is now the first part of the eucharistic celebration, is the final blossoming of what had become the liturgy of the synagogue at the time of Christ. This, in turn, is seen by Judaism as making its first appearance and disclosing its full meaning in the ninth and tenth chapters of Nehemiah. There we find the scribe Ezra, after the return of the exiles, in a Jerusalem still desolated, which they are trying to rebuild. He gathers the people on the site of the ruined Temple, and reads to them the whole of the five Books of Moses, the permanent nucleus of their Bible and ours. These had just been definitively compiled by his fellow scribes during the captivity. They had done this to prepare for the new gathering and rebuilding on the basis of a renewed faith in the saving deeds of God in the past, now to prolong itself into the faith in God's readiness to repair, to restore, and ultimately to fulfill the hope of Israel.

Now they hear together the whole great epic of creation and salvation—the initial fall of man, who is made after God's image; the election and separation of Abraham; then the similar separation and exodus of the children of Abraham, freed from material and spiritual captivity out of Egypt to be brought through the desert land to the land of promise, the land where they would be at home with God, who has become *their* God, and they a people after God's own heart.

That reading, however, since it concluded with the solemn warnings and promises of Moses in Deuteronomy, could not but make them interpret their own exile and return from captivity as a new Exodus. Again the people of God, having been thrown into the crucible of such a trial, at last are to be disengaged, as a true and faithful remnant, from the mass of unbelievers, and gathered into a newly built Jerusalem, there to serve God forever in his perfect service.

This reading was not for them a pious remembrance of the past. They heard it at this precise moment in their personal and individual history. It made clear to them that the God who had spoken to their fathers all through that history was speaking to them in the same way, in a manner still more decisive here and now. Here was the gathering together of a renewed and perfected people of God, having had its faith put to the test, in order to build together with God, not only Jerusalem, but a temple, *the* temple of the living God now and forever living in men fully alive.

Soon, however—we see this in the Book of Haggai—the reconstructed city, the rededicated Temple, far from being the perfect city and the eternal temple expected, were but a shadow of the former city and the glory of its Temple. The faithful remnant had not been purified and refined into the faithful servant of the second Isaiah. Therefore, the conversion of the Gentiles and the renewal of the earth and heavens was still to be expected from a Son of Man who must come down from the rent heavens to this earth of ours so that the coming of the kingdom of heaven itself in its one true king might be fulfilled indeed, now and forever.

And it was to prepare Isaiah for *that*—that on every Sabbath the reading of the law and the prophets, in the synagogue assemblies, had to be pursued until the coming of him who should come; and so that he should come and come quickly. This, at the time of Jesus, was the expectation of the most faithful Jews taking part in the synagogue service, and this was the expectation he was intended to fulfill.

Think, now, no longer of the assembly of liberated exiles on Mount Zion gathered around Ezra the scribe, but of the people; as St. Luke says, "expecting the consolation of Israel," gathered in the synagogue at Nazareth around Jesus. He sits down in "the chair of Moses," where the rabbis sat to explain and apply the promises and demands addressed to them by God through Moses and the prophets. Jesus has just read the sixty-first chapter of the Book of Isaiah: "The Spirit of the Lord is upon me because he has anointed me to preach good news to the poor; he has sent me to proclaim release to the captives and recovering of sight to the blind, to set at liberty those who are oppressed, to proclaim the acceptable year of the Lord."

Jesus returns the book to the minister, the eyes of all in the synagogue are fixed on him. They await his comment. He says: "Today this scripture has been fulfilled in your hearing. . . ."

Think of that page of the Gospel, read in this perspective, the perspective of the whole development of the Bible, of the word of God, of the history of salvation. Visualize the event which is the liturgy of the word of God in our eucharistic celebration in these terms, and in it see the function of the priest among us.

The priest is, as every Christian should be, a witness to his brethren, Christian or not, of the dynamic reality of the progressive development, of the ultimate actuality of that word of God. The priest has to be, in addition, not only an expert, able by his intellectual formation to explain what the word of God, humanly, historically, and cosmically means, but also a *messenger* of the one catholic and apostolic Church of all ages and countries, mandated by it to tell his local church gathered here and now, what indeed, in its common experience, the experience of all the saints, that word has actually meant. Above all, a priest, by his ordination, has been identified with the continuation all through the ages of the apostolic community of ministry gathered by Jesus himself, to be sent to man, as he had been sent by the Father. The priest, in the gathering of the believers, is for them the visible sign of the continued presence of Christ to tell them, still with his own authority: "Today this scripture has been fulfilled in your hearing. . . ."

Even if he is a poor preacher, even if he is a worthless tool, the priest in the eucharistic assembly, speaking to us as one of those who have been sent to us by Christ in the same way as Christ had been sent by the Father, is the permanent attestation that the word of God, coming to say its last word in the Gospel of Jesus Christ, is not only a word of light, but the word of life, the presence, the perfect presence, the permanent presence of God with us in Christ. This present word of life takes hold not only of our minds but of our whole being, to bring us not only to a full consciousness of his design concerning us but to the fulfillment of that design in us, through us, and with us. It is in the nature of the divine word to be action, to be creative. Its supreme creation is to evoke a response in the heart of man, a response not merely of belief, but of obedience and love, to create a totally renewed humanity for the total renewal of the world.

Now comes the natural, the unavoidable transition from the liturgy of the word to the sacramental liturgy, to the eucharistic prayer which constitutes the consecration of the Eucharist.

Here again we have in the great assembly around Ezra on Mount Zion a first sketch of what that prayer was to be. It was a response of man to the word of God to him, evoked from the depths of his heart by the creative power of that selfsame word.

When the whole history of salvation comes at last to its conclusion, the elders of the people led by Ezra break forth into a hymn of exultant praise to God, who first created heaven and earth in all their glory, and made man in his own image to submit creation to the full design of its maker. Then they praise him that once man had forfeited his vocation, God has not abandoned him, but through patriarchs and prophets, trial and deliverance, drawn a faithful people out of an unfaithful race. Then the praise of the Creator and Savior God turns to a supplication which is the natural outcome of that praise. Now that God is near the completion of his promises, may he, as in the past, grant us to be gathered together in his faithful city, the new Jerusalem, to rebuild his final temple, when all creation reconciled around his elect will glorify him forever.

As the gathering of the people returned from exile to hear the word of God was the pattern of the future synagogue services of meditation on the word, so the rehearsal of this prayer, a fully developed *berakah* ("blessing"), the eucharistic praise and thanksgiving for the progressive realization of the design of God, was to be forever the continuity of the synagogue prayers. In it the people, having come to maturity, acknowledged all that God had done and was still doing to bring them to achieve in their own history the realization of his own design for them and for the whole world. And the concluding prayer, since it was for that fulfillment which would mean God in every being, was a self-surrender, a collective consecration to whatever that fulfillment might imply for them, so that all God's creation might live only to his praise and glory.

At the center of these supplications was a prayer, borrowed from the liturgy of the Temple for the consecration of all the sacrifices of Israel so that his people, in them and through them, may be raised to God's presence and become a perfect offering.

However, toward the end of the Old Testament period, when messianic expectation reached its highest pitch, we see—as at Qumran—a select group; as St. Luke puts it, "those who were waiting for the consolation of Israel," considered as better than the formal Temple offering, the gathering of a community of faithful believers in the nearness of the fulfillment of the messianic promises, around the table of their community meal, on the eve of a Sabbath or a feast day.

As these gatherings were opened by the fraction and the sharing of all in the one bread, they were concluded by drinking from one cup of wine solemnly blessed by the head of the community. But in that Eucharist of the meal, as it was called, we find again in shortened form the great *berakah* following the hearing of God's word. However, this time it is not just the light of the knowledge of God which is the central theme of the prayer, but rather the life found in this presence with his own.

A most interesting and important feature of the prayer was a special insertion for a Sabbath or a feast day. It centered on the idea of the "memorial." In the case of the meal, the food reminded the people of the creation of life, and the land which had produced the food reminded them of salvific history, of which they were the heirs. So now they say to God: "Let this memorial of your own people, of your high deeds in the past of the promised Messiah and the expected Kingdom arise, be accepted in Your Presence, and may we be introduced together with it into all that You have promised and we expect in faith."

As Jeremias, the German exegete, has shown, the "memorial" in Jewish liturgy, as in the whole Bible, is not just a subjective reminder; it is a token given to us by God himself of the permanence in the present of his saving acts in the past, of their continuing activity in our midst. But even more important, the "memorial" is given us by God to be re-presented to *him,* to remind him of his promises, so that we may be sure to be accepted when we supplicate him for the final fulfillment in us and for us of his loving will.

All this brings us inevitably to Jesus, at the end of the meal, taking the one bread, blessing it, and breaking it as his body was to be broken for us and given to us to make us one body; and also to his blessing the last cup, as the communion in his blood which will introduce us into his new and everlasting covenant. Henceforth, that meal was to become the "memorial," no longer of the preparatory saving deeds of God in the Old Covenant, but of his cross and resurrection, as the fulfillment of all the images and promises. As St. Paul was to comment: "Every time therefore you eat of that bread and drink of that cup, you proclaim the death of the Lord until he comes." This means, as Jeremias has shown: "Every time you eat of that bread and drink of that cup you remind God of the death of his son, *so that* he comes.".—so that the parousia takes place which shall be the consummation of all things.

Here we can say that as Christ appears in the Gospel as the perfect word of God to man, in his divine life become human, as the Son of God become the Son of Man, so at the summit of his human life, he becomes perfect Eucharist, the perfect surrender of man to the loving will of God, in one definitive sacrifice of praise.

Just as the priest in the first part of the celebration appears as the representative of the head *to* the body, to bring to its members the fullness of the presence and the creative and redemptive activity of God, given in the word made man; so the priest in the second part of the celebration appears as the representative of the head *in* the body, in the solemn rehearsal of the eucharistic prayer and self-oblation of Christ, in and for his body the Church, to make it possible for all the members of Christ to be consummated in their unity with him, their unity in him, their common self-offering to the loving obedience of his only Son.

When we see the priest in the midst of his brothers in Christ celebrating the Eucharist with them, it should be manifest that this ministerial priesthood, the sacramental sign in our midst of the one priesthood of Christ, far from making useless or void the royal priesthood of all believers, has no other meaning or object but to make it fully actualized. In fact, the two fundamental priestly actions of the minister: his proclamation of the word, his consecration and distribution of the Eucharist, are deprived of content and meaning if they are not seen in their necessary connection with the three priestly actions of the whole body of Christ, constantly described by the Fathers as praying, offering, and communicating.

The proclamation of the word in its full actualization of the presence of Christ in our midst as the Living Word would be meaningless were it not to create the response of faith, exultant praise, and confident expectation which is properly the prayer of the faithful. That prayer, that response, evoked by the word itself, also has to lead to a total surrender of our human nature, of all our actions. This the faithful will express in offering the bread and wine, as their whole being and life, to be taken into its very source. However, this surrender would be ineffective were it not taken by Christ, consecrated and assimilated to his own sacrifice, through his own eucharistic prayer which the priest utters—once again, as Christ's own sacerdotal prayer as the head, in and for the body. But again, that consecration itself, of our food and drink into the body and the blood of Christ, into the very source of the new life, would be meaningless were it not to lead to the communion of all: to our being personally and collectively renewed in our actual membership in Christ's own body, to penetrate the whole world with the new and eternal life of the resurrected Christ, to the glory of the Father, in the power of the Spirit.

In this sense, the Christian priest, of all men, is to be fully a "man for others," as the minister of the headship of the body. Just as Christ did not die to dispense us from suffering and dying, but to make us able to die as he only could die, to kill death, and to manifest in man and in the whole creation the life of God himself; so the priest, a shepherd following the Good Shepherd along that way that he alone could tread, leads Christ's flock, through the word and the great sacrament of the cross, into the fullness of life.

chapter 12

THE PRIEST AS PROFESSIONAL

F. H. Borsch

I well remember an incident that took place shortly after I had been ordained. I was visiting an elderly parishioner who had recently entered the hospital. After we had talked awhile and prayed together, she thanked me for visiting. She then added, "But I suppose it is your job to come see me, isn't it?" For the first time I knew from the tone of her voice and the look in her eyes what it meant to be a "professional" in the less valued sense of the word. She was still glad I had come, but it was indeed my job to be there. I was paid to come visit her, and somehow this seemed to make our relationship less personal and meaningful from her point of view.

The experience has not been isolated. A casual conversation at a party will gradually come to test the waters of more serious discussion. Finally there comes a sincere and searching question: "Do you really believe in a personal God?" As I reply in the affirmative, I again see that withdrawing look in the eyes: "Oh yes, of course! He's a priest. He has to say that." Again I am a professional.

In this sense, ordained persons may understandably find the word "professional" not much to their liking. Priests may wish to protest that they are not paid all that much for this work (in some cases not at all) and that it was not for the money that they became priests in the first place. It may be well outside normal working hours as they are making their hospital calls, with no one checking up to see whether they are doing or saying the right thing. Besides, priests may wish to reflect, they are really acting on behalf of the entire Christian community which supports them as they visit the sick and answer the inquirer. Yet, no matter how much much one protests, the priest is wise who understands and takes seriously the awareness that ordained persons are regarded in many of their words and actions as professionals—people who do much of what they do either because they are paid to do so or

111

because it is a responsibility of their office or for both reasons. This perception of the ordained person represents a truth that the individual priest must learn to live with and through.

II

The word has more favorable connotations, however. The professional person is one who is trained and educated for his or her work. To be called a professional can mean that a person is regarded as reliable and well capable of carrying out particular functions. To this person one can go with assurance that the individual will have knowledge and the wisdom of experience.

But the work of most priests is highly variegated in character, and this has caused some uncertainty and even quandary in an era of increasing specialization. Explicitly or implicitly a number of priests have questioned their professionalism in the sense that we are now using the word. Perceiving themselves to be jacks of several trades but masters of none, some priests have chosen the route of increasing specialization as a way of maintaining a professional stance. Many positive developments have resulted from this movement as ordained persons have been able to grow in skill areas and to contribute these capabilities as members of team ministries or through individual practice.

In the last several years, however, there has been a rebirth of the awareness of the place of the generalist in society. In medical, legal, academic, and other professional fields the need is felt for persons who are good at doing a number of related tasks and who have understanding and appreciation for them in their interrelationship. This development has already had some effect on educational programs in these fields. One can well believe that this renewed sense of the need for and value of the generalist will help to foster among priests a heightened feeling for the importance of their work as professionals. No doubt in the future, as before, individual priests will be better at doing some things than others; but, with the growth in the realization that people want to relate to persons with a broader sense of life's interconnectedness, the priest may better understand breadth of skills as a strength and not a weakness.

Throughout the history of the Christian ordained ministry there has been a fair degree of fluidity in the understanding of the variety of roles which the priest is to perform for and on behalf of the community. Certainly in our highly pluralistic contemporary world expectations of priests vary considerably. Also, because of the very interrelatedness of the tasks of priesthood, one cannot easily categorize functions of ministry. In the daily life and ministrations of a priest these functions inter-thread, thereby affecting the very texture of the other roles. For our purposes, however, we can describe briefly five major areas of priestly endeavor for which expectations of professional competence are usually to be found.

The priest is a teacher, and a teacher of many things. The priest is to know the model revelations—the stories which give form to and unite the many Christian communities throughout the world. This individual should understand the Bible from the perspective of those who first experienced its sayings and stories in order effectively to guide the interpretation of contemporary Christian inspiration. The teacher-priest should know the history of Christianity in a manner that helps others to be free for the future—strong in the awareness that there have been, and therefore can be, many different ways in which the Church may be organized and act for mission, ministry, and worship.

The teacher-priest must be a theologian of the common life. One of the great values of a theological education is its enhancement of perspective, enabling one so educated to teach the same truth in different ways instead of knowing only one way of approaching a Christian view of life. The priest as teacher is able to help individuals from a variety of backgrounds of experience to reflect in their own terms upon their lives as lived in the presence of God. As a contemporary teacher, the professional priest will have sufficient knowledge of such disciplines as psychology and sociology as to appreciate their applicability to an understanding of human growth and development. There is a reasonable expectation that the priest will know how people learn.

Among the vital concerns of the priest will be the teaching and sharing of insights regarding prayer. The ordained person should have both knowledge and experience of varying approaches to the awareness of God in human life in order to be a companion and guide to others in their growth and development. In this area as in others, the priest, for the purposes of Christian mission, is to be a teacher of those who are themselves in their own ways to be teachers and witnesses to others.

Closely related and often integral to the priest's role as teacher is that of proclaimer or preacher. Here especially the priest is to make available for use the insights gained from the community-shared stories of the Bible in order that they might become cause for creating and interpreting new insight and revelation. As one who is a pilgrim and witness, the priest is to search out new stories or parables by means of which the themes of biblical parables can find contemporary expression. As a herald of the new possibilities of the kingdom which Jesus announced, the priest is also to be a prophet—pointing to ethical imperatives and seeking to make sure that the word of God will be heard at the same time as a word of judgment and grace, hope and challenge. In terms of this role, too, the professionalism of the priest can be increased through experience, practice, and learning from the insights of others.

A third role of the priest is that of steward of the sacraments. With theological understanding and sensitivity—with awareness of the meaning of symbols and liturgical acts—the priest is to give leadership in the presentation of sacramental, life-interpreting activities. For and on behalf of the community, the ordained leader is to be a focal person for this vital witness. Without the effective drama of sacramental gesture and event people can quickly become rootless and out of touch with the profound meanings of a life which is at once bodily, psychic, and spiritual.

The priest is normally called upon to be a counselor in a variety of situations, especially to be an individual who is with other people to help them in the hard spots of life. The wise and professional priest learns how to develop a number of counseling approaches to suit different circumstances and people, recognizing a time to listen creatively and a time to advise, being aware of opportunities to teach and opportunities to allow those being counseled to teach themselves. The professional priest as counselor will also have further resources near at hand (in the persons of psychiatrists, social workers, and others) and be alert to the need for them.

One of the chief functions of the priest as counselor is to be a reconciler, one who seeks to make peace and also to pronounce healing words of forgiveness and new acceptance and hope. In this way the priest is to carry the Christian ministry of healing to the minds and the emotions of men and women. Sometimes the new health and freedom so engendered will extend to healings of the body as well.

A fifth professional role of the priest is that of administrator. Many priests will be expected to be competent in helping communities of Christians to organize themselves for ministry and mission. A vital work of the ordained ministry is this form of giving assistance and support to others in their ministries.

Since we are living in a society and a decade which is understandably suspicious of many styles of leadership and forms of institutions, it is not surprising that a number of priests, as well as those planning to be priests, tend to minimize the need for institutions and, at least outwardly, also to eschew roles of leadership for themselves. But rarely in the course of human events is it a question of whether there should be institutions and leadership for certain purposes, but rather what kinds of institutions. There is a sense in which Jesus could even be said to have formed the first men's club. The disciples seem to have recognized his leadership and there are references in the New Testament to economic arrangements made for the support and furtherance of their work.

It may well be that simpler and less hierarchical organizations will better serve Christian communities in the future. Certainly it would be helpful if the contemporary Church were less engaged in maintenance and more in service and mission. Yet to accomplish this very goal will require leadership from men and women who have developed abilities for encouraging community self-awareness and decision-making, conflict management, eliciting commitment, and the sharing of personal resources. It is to be hoped that these leaders will also have grown in the spirit of servanthood in order to have moved beyond merely manipulative skills. They will need to know themselves well enough to begin to deal with their own propensities to control others—especially through the subtle instruments of moral and spiritual authority. Not all of this leadership will or should come from the clergy, but there is a proper expectation that priests should have studied and worked to develop these and other administrative and leadership talents in a professional manner.

III

A third way of understanding the word "professional" is closer to its root meaning; a professional is a professed person, someone whose very life publicly declares certain values and commitments. So we speak of individuals professing vows and of members of a religious order as being professed.

This sense of the word reminds us of two fundamental and related characteristics vital to any true priesthood. Standing in and behind the several roles of priesthood described above, there must be a person who is known in these roles and is accessible through them. In addition, the power for Christian faith is best manifested when there is such integrity between the person and the enacted roles as to bring integration to the roles and the character of personal conviction to their practice.

Behind the new movement that has revalued the place of the generalist in professional fields, one can detect strong sociological and psychological factors. People do not regularly wish to be treated as though made up of many different parts which can be dealt with separately and objectively. Specialization has its obvious uses and merits, but people also wish for relationship with professional individuals on a person-to-person basis.

For theological reasons the significance of this awareness must be especially stressed for the practice of the Christian ministry. Again and again the New Testament witnesses to the understanding that God's chosen means for revealing and sharing himself in the world is human persons. Christians believe this to have been accomplished decisively in Jesus. There seemed in him to be an extraordinary integrity between his words and his actions. This was why he was remembered as having taught with such power. He did not just tell parables, he did them, standing in and behind his words. In a very real sense he was the Good Samaritan showing what it could mean to be free enough not to have to ask the negative and legalistic question: "Who is my neighbor?" In this sense Jesus is for Christians the preeminent professed person and the model for any professional ministry which is to be done in the "imitation of Christ." In his ministry as teacher, proclaimer, and prophet, celebrant of his own self-offering, healer and counselor, and—yes—administrator and leader for his little community, Jesus was authentically and uniquely present as a person.

We become aware, then, that the essence of the profession of priesthood is to be found in the development and offering of the gifts of personhood. It is through persons that God most intends to be present in the world, and priests best represent the God that is Jesus-like through their ministerial roles when they themselves are seeking to be present to others. It is for this reason above all that we can never expect to be able fully to define or describe priesthood. With its rootedness through the personhood of Jesus in God, priesthood is ultimately a mystery. All our attempts at definition and description must be understood to fall short, for we do not yet know all that God intends persons, or persons as priests, to be. In the context of this awareness, and while acting as a focus for the ministry of all Christians, the one who would serve as priest must seek so to give of the true self as to move through and beyond any mere professionalism toward the profession of the full Christian life.

chapter 13

THE PRIEST AS AUTHORITY ON THE WORLD

John M. Gessell

Religiousness, says Kierkegaard, is suffering. The capacity to feel and to be moved deeply is the sign of that compassion, springing from the unique vision of faith, which is the mark of true religion and points to its authority wherever it is exercised.

The unparalleled quality of compassionate anguish is perfectly revealed in Tom Wicker's account of the Attica Prison uprising of September, 1971.* Wicker has elsewhere observed that he has no special competence or expertise in prison management or prison reform, but his compassionate involvement, driven by an unquestionable loyalty to his own sense of humanity, has made him an unarguable authority on the American penal system.

Wicker wrote that for most of his life he had lived by the reporter's peculiar standards, the ethic of the press box rather than of the participant. It was high time, he thought, that he hold himself to a line. What was a life if it was never put to challenge, not just by foolhardy choice but as a logical and perhaps inevitable consequence of the way a person has lived and believed?

Wicker was one of a small group of men that the rebelling inmates requested be sent to the prison as observers. The exact position of this group was never made clear, and as the time passed, their power diminished to the vanishing point. As negotiators they were helpless. As advisors they were unanimously reluctant to suggest that the prisoners commit themselves one way or another. All they could hope for was to buy time in the event that some form of peaceful agreement could be reached. Even here they were unsuccessful.

A Time to Die (New York: Quadrangle/The New York Times Co., 1975).

And so it was inevitable that their effort would fail, for neither the community of Attica, nor, indeed, the American community outside its walls, was prepared to admit either its responsibilities or its failures with regard to the prisoners. This experience did, however, force Wicker to confront a problem which he has now made the concern of us all. Wicker's compassion testifies to a passionate religious conviction, and this compassion commands him to share the heartbreak and devastation of the brokenness of the human experience as disclosed at Attica. He has shown us what it takes to be an authority on the world.

Authority is born out of this sort of authentic religious compassion. It inheres in the ineffable quality of religious suffering, not suffering for its own sake but suffering through participation in the suffering of the world and the world's anguish. Authority on the world is conferred upon him who is willing to suffer for the world. The authority of religiousness, then, does not lie in its superior knowledge or in its exemplary behavior, but it is inherent in its commitment, its openness to suffering, its capacity for compassion for the world. This has important implications for priestly authority on the world.

The priest has no inherent authority either in himself or in his office. Along with all baptized Christians, authority may emerge out of his experience with the world and fasten itself upon him. This authority arises from his willingness to suffer, to be stung by the world's need, from his capacity for compassion. In addition, an authority is conferred upon him by the Church for the exercise of specialized functions on its behalf. These two sources of Christian authority are interrelated, as we shall see, but both are rooted in the one Gospel.

The priest has no authority other than that inherent in the Gospel. The authority of the priest, as the shared authority of any baptized Christian, is the authority of one who bears the Gospel in the world and who is enabled thereby to perceive the world compassionately and authoritatively in its light. The authority conferred upon him, on the other hand, by his ordination in the Church through the power of the Spirit, is carried out by the Church in obedience to the Gospel. This twofold authority is rooted in the one Gospel and is responsive to the authoritative word of God. This word goes forth as a creative and reconstitutive power. It confers in turn the power of critical discrimination, the power of imagination and perception, and the power for reconciliation and reconstruction. In what follows, I shall examine the authority of the priest on the world as the authority of baptism, the authority of the Eucharist, and the authority of reconstruction.

THE AUTHORITY OF BAPTISM

In what, then, lies the distinctive authority of the priest on the world? He has no unique authority, but shares in the common authority of all baptized members of the body of Christ. The calculation of the relationship between Gospel and world is, to paraphrase T. S. Eliot, an occupation for a saint. It is shared by all baptized Christians as command and grace. But the validity of Christian priesthood is, in part, guaranteed by the priest's own conformity to this authenticating task. The exercise of Christian authority on the world is a part of priestly formation, and a repeatedly authenticating act.

If priestly authority on the world is, in part, constituted by the exercise of perception through the unique angle of vision of the Gospel, seeing the world constituted and reconstituted through the eyes of faith, there are three moments constitutive of this authority. These moments are compassion, alienation, and vision. They are not, however, related dialectically, but synchronously. They are experienced altogether at the same time as responses of baptismal faith.

In the compassion born of the vision of faith, the priest weeps with Jesus over Jerusalem and its rejection of the prophetic vision of the Gospel. His compassion is extended to the broken world and he shares in that pain. He knows the anguish of our troubled, crooked human nature. He experiences the shame of our errors and ignorances in judgment and in charity; he suffers the embarrassment and guilt of our negligences and of our sinful behavior. He is slow to judge, and he issues that judgment without condemnation; he is swift to forgive and assures that forgiveness, commending the sinner to the throne of grace and mercy, without commending the sin. He is swift to offer acceptance and the support of the outstretched hand of love which demands nothing in return. The priest knows his own experience of brokenness and lives with his own bent nature.

The priest shares in the alienation of Christians because the authority of the Gospel is alienating inasmuch as the Gospel appears as alien to a fallen world. Christians are not to be conformed to the world, though their consciousness needs to be formed by the need of the world. But this need is also alien because the fall has darkened the eye of understanding and perception, and the world does not know its own need. Further, the Christian is an alien in the world and shares in the world's own alienation because the contingent structures of the created world have been elevated into the idolatrous objects of our corrupt imaginations, and have taken on the meaning of self-authenticating objects constituting a power now at enmity with the kingdom of God. The principalities and powers of the world are in rebellion and Christians

may lose their way among them, becoming estranged from themselves
and from God. The reification of the world through its own imagination
into the pretension of ultimate power leads it to make idolatrous claims
which Christians are bound to reject. And so they become alien for
Christ's sake and the Gospel's, even as Christ himself was outcast and
an alien to the world that put him on a cross.

The authority of Christian priesthood, then, is realized in the exercise
of that healing and reconstituting compassion for the world, which, at
the same time, does not suffer the confusion of being conformed to the
world. The authority of priesthood on the world arises in turn from the
priest's ability to remain alien from the world and to render a responsible critique of the world in the light of his vision of faith. The moments
of compassion and of alienation are complemented by vision. The cross
of Christ provides a unique angle of vision on the world. In the light of
the cross and the resurrection faith, the world is refracted in a singular
way. And the priest calls and recalls the world back to this vision, a
vision which heals and transcends the brokenness of the world. For he
knows that the idolatrousness of the human situation and the brokenness of the world are not the final but the penultimate words. The
authority of priesthood is in the acknowledgment and the proclamation
of the finality of the creative and the reconstituting word of the Gospel
that is known and grasped in the unique vision of faith which sees the
world reconciled and whole.

The authority of priesthood on the world is constituted by the exercise of that authority in the moments of compassion, alienation, and
vision. These acts are signs of the healing power of the Gospel, and assist
in bringing to the world that healing power in obedience and in loyalty
to the God of faith. In sum, part of the authority of the priest on the
world is that of Christian baptism, sharing the pain of abandonment and
hopelessness where it is experienced in the interstices of disorder and
despair; or, as Bonhoeffer put it, participating in the sufferings of God
in the world.

THE AUTHORITY OF EUCHARIST

The authority of the priest on the world is amplified by ordination to
a sacramental ministry of Eucharist, of showing forth the Lord's death
until his coming again. This at once dignifies and heals suffering. The
Church confers this authority of the Gospel on the priest, both on its
own behalf and for the sake of the world.

Christian priesthood is forged out of the unique experience of the
Christian community. The priest's authority on the world is that of the
one who convenes eucharistic community for the recalling of the sal-

vific event through which Christ redeemed and liberated the world, overcoming the enmity between God and man, and by leading that community into liturgical participation in that efficacious event.

This action, authorized by the Church through ordination, declares God's unequivocal purpose to save and to reconstitute the world. It is also an unequivocal call to action to attack with compassion every center of power, in the Church as in the state, in the person as in the family, which constitutes itself alien to God's purposes. The authority of the priest on the world is conferred by the Church and is centered in the Eucharist as the Gospel declaration of the purpose of God ultimately to overcome all human fallibility and to knit together the broken world.

Thus eucharistic authority, shared by the Christian community, is the authority to declare to itself and to the world both God's judgment and his healing power. This dual eucharistic authority is in principle indivisible, for the two actions of healing and judging coinhere. At the same time, eucharistic action both divides and unites. It divides idolatrous power from God's purposive power, and it unites sinful humanity with God's redeeming grace.

The authority of the priest on the world, then, centers in his authority, conferred upon him by the Church, to convene eucharistic community. This action is pivotal since it is both the source and the center for compassionate suffering as well as the healing balm for the world's need. Thus, in the Eucharist all compassion and suffering are gathered in and made one with our oblations whereby we experience the healing of our suffering and of our brokenness. We experience the wholeness of the resurrected Lord truly present to us.

The authority on the world of the priest as baptized Christian is gathered up and completed in the authoritative action of the priest as eucharistic officer. From here the priest's authority on the world moves out again from the eucharistic action as the shared authority of all Christians called to go forth again into the broken world. The picture here is that of shared authority brought from the world to the holy table, offered by the priest in eucharistic action on behalf of the whole body, issuing forth again as the shared authority of all baptized Christians and going back into the world bearing the Gospel in the grace and power of the Eucharist.

THE AUTHORITY OF RECONSTRUCTION

The authority of baptism and the authority of the Eucharist are completed in reconstruction. Faith that issues in compassion and prayer inevitably leads to action. The central and unassailable fact which Christianity addresses is the tragic dimension of the world. The central and unassailable message which Christianity brings is that the way of God is the way beyond the tragedy of the human experience. Identity with the cross of Christ is at the same time solidarity with the world and with the poor and the sinful, with the broken and the oppressed people of the world.

The authority of the Gospel confers the power of criticism and judgment, of imagination and perception, and of the vision of reconstruction. All of these are born out of the struggle of compassion and alienation, supported by the vision of faith, and nurtured in the Eucharist. In this way the world is seen anew through the perspective of faith. It is seen in the light of its transcendent reference, without which it has no meaning. This vision of faith constitutes the authority of reconstruction. Here the priest's authority on the world is that of the diagnostician. This is the authority of one who feels and sees the reconstituted world, and of the theological critic, the maker of new knowledge of and for the world.

The last and completing action of the priest as authority on the world is, therefore, the inescapable call to attack with compassion those powers existing in the world contrary to the kingdom of God wherever they are found. For the centers of worldly power are always at odds with the reign of God. The authority of the priest on the world is, with Christians everywhere, to attack the idolatrous powers of the world which are at enmity with God's purposes and his kingdom.

The authenticating power of suffering, of Eucharist, is not completed without the authenticating power of prophetic judgment and disclosure. Without this, compassion and suffering are trivialized, and the Eucharist becomes blasphemous. Since Eucharist implies both healing and discriminate judgment, the priest as authority on the world is, together with all Christians everywhere, inescapably and consequentially involved in the compassionate confrontation, for example, of institutionalized violence, of attacks on privacy, of structural and systematic causes of poverty, and of economic and social injustice and oppression wherever they occur in the world. And the same confrontation must be had within our own household of faith, with our complicity in the violence and the injustice of the world, and with our inability to come to terms with the problems of authority, ordination, and human sexuality.

CONCLUSION

The priest has no inherent authority on the world. His authority is that of any baptized Christian whose authority is inherent in his own compassionate suffering. The priest's authority on the world is either conferred upon him by this right of suffering, or by the intention of the Church that declares in him its own eucharistic priesthood in accordance with its apprehension of the Christian experience in the world. In other words, the experience of struggling with the relationship between Gospel and world and with the authenticating vision of faith is a validating act. It is this authority, garnered out of personal Christian experience in the struggle with faith and belief, and out of the Church's existence in the world, that is validated in ordination.

Finally, as Tom Wicker points out, the authentication of authority is the inevitable consequence of the way a person lives and believes. We are to go out into the world with gladness and singleness of heart.

chapter 14

"BECAUSE BESET WITH WEAKNESS . . ."

Michael J. Buckley

There is a tendency among us Americans, common and obvious enough, recommended by common sense and successful practice, to estimate a person's aptitude for a profession or for a career by listing his strengths. Jane speaks well, possesses an able mind, exhibits genuine talents for leadership and debate; she would be an excellent lawyer. John has recognizably good judgment, a scientific turn of interest, obvious manual dexterity, and deep human concerns; he would make a splendid surgeon.

The tendency is to transfer this method of evaluation to the priesthood, to estimate a man by his gifts and talents, to line up his positive achievements and his capacity for more, to understand his promise for the future in terms of his accomplishments in the past, and to make the call within his life contingent on the attainments of personality or grace. Because a man is religiously serious, prayerful, socially adept, intellectually perceptive; possesses interior integrity, sound common sense, and habits of hard work—therefore he will make a fine priest.

I think that transfer is disastrous. There is a different question, one proper to the priesthood as of its very essence, if not uniquely proper to it: Is this man weak enough to be a priest? Is this man deficient enough so that he cannot ward off significant suffering from his life, so that he lives with a certain amount of failure, so that he feels what it is to be an average man? Is there any history of confusion, of self-doubt, of interior anguish? Has he had to deal with fear, come to terms with frustrations, or accept deflated expectations? These are critical questions and they probe for weakness. Why? Because, according to Hebrews, it is in this deficiency, in this interior lack, in this weakness, that the efficacy of the ministry and priesthood of Christ lies.

125

"For because he himself has suffered and been tempted, he is able to help those who are tempted. . . . For we have not a high priest who is unable to sympathize with our weaknesses, but one who in every respect has been tempted as we are, yet without sinning. . . . He can deal gently with the ignorant and wayward since he himself is beset with weakness" (Hebrews 2:18; 4:15; 5:2).

How critically important it is for us to enter into the seriousness of this revelation, of this conjunction between priesthood and weakness, that we dwell upon deficiency as part of our vocation! Otherwise we can secularize our lives into an amalgam of desires and talents; and we can feel our weakness as a threat to our priesthood, as indicative that we should rethink what was previously resolved, as symptomatic that we were never genuinely called, that we do not have the resources to complete what we once thought was our destiny and which once spoke to our generosity and fidelity.

What do I mean by weakness? Not the experience of sin; almost its opposite. Weakness is the experience of a peculiar liability to suffering, a profound sense of inability both to do and to protect: an inability, even after great effort, to author, to perform as we should want, to affect what we had determined, to succeed with the completeness that we might have hoped. It is this openness to suffering which issues in the inability to secure our own future, to protect ourselves from any adversity, to live with easy clarity and assurance; or to ward off shame, pain, or even interior anguish.

If a man is clever enough or devious enough or poised enough, he can limit his horizons and expectations and accomplish pretty much what he would want. He can secure his perimeters and live without a sense of ineffectual efforts, a feeling of failure or inadequacy or of shame before what might have been. But if he cannot—either because of his history or his temperament or his task—then he experiences weakness at the heart of his life. And this experience, rather than militating against his priesthood, is part of its essential structure. This liability to suffering forms a critically important indication of the call of God, that terrible sinking sense of incapacity before the mission of Moses and the vocation of Jeremiah, that profound conviction of sinfulness when the vision of God rose before Isaiah and demanded response.

There is a classic comparison running through contemporary philosophy between Socrates and Christ, a judgment between them in human excellence. Socrates went to his death with calmness and poise. He accepted the judgment of the court, discoursed on the alternatives suggested by death and on the dialectical indications of immortality, found no cause for fear, drank the poison, and died. Jesus—how much the contrary. Jesus was almost hysterical with terror and fear; "with loud cries and tears to him who was able to save him from death." He looked repeatedly to his friends for comfort and prayed for an escape from death, and he found neither. Finally he established control over himself and moved into his death in silence and lonely isolation, even into the terrible interior suffering of the hidden divinity, the absence of God.

I once thought that this was because Socrates and Jesus suffered different deaths, the one so much more terrible than the other, the pain and agony of the cross so overshadowing the release of the hemlock. But now I think that this explanation, though correct as far as it runs, is superficial and secondary. Now I believe that Jesus was a more profoundly weak man than Socrates, more liable to physical pain and weariness, more sensitive to human rejection and contempt, more affected by love and hate. Socrates never wept over Athens. Socrates never expressed sorrow and pain over the betrayal of friends. He was possessed and integral, never overextended, convinced that the just man could never suffer genuine hurt. And for this reason, Socrates—one of the greatest and most heroic men who has ever existed, a paradigm of what humanity can achieve within the individual—was a philosopher. And for the same reason, Jesus of Nazareth was a priest—ambiguous, suffering, mysterious, and salvific.

So with us, a priest must also be liable to suffering, weak because he must become like what he touches—the body of Christ. Obviously the ordinary person understands priest primarily and imaginatively through the Eucharist within the Church. And what is this Eucharist? The body of Christ? Yes, certainly, but how understood? How does Christ conceive and present this, his body? This is an important question, for psychologists maintain that a man evaluates himself in terms of his spontaneous body-images, that what he senses and feels about his body is what he senses and feels about himself, that as he perceives his body so he perceives himself.

How then does Christ perceive this, his body? A body which was broken for us. A blood which was shed for us. He understands himself as a sacrificed self, effective only passing through his destruction, giving life and freedom only because he himself has moved through death and terror and achieved new life. In our Mass, when we celebrate "the great mystery which he has left us," the Eucharist only achieves its graced entrance into our lives if it is broken and distributed. Thus it is the liability of Christ to suffering, his ability to be broken and shed, that makes his priesthood effective and his Eucharist possible. How paradoxical this mystery is! The strength of our priesthood lies precisely in the weakness which seems to threaten it. The sensitivity and openness to discouragement and suffering are constitutive of the mystery of the priesthood itself.

Weakness relates us profoundly with other people. It allows us to feel with them the human condition, the human struggle and darkness and anguish which call out for salvation. For to be a human being is to take a certain amount of suffering into life. It is hard to get at this consideration, since so much in Western civilization attempts to disguise it or affects to despise it. One of the most debilitating aspects of American society is that we do not authentically admit the cost in a struggle and almost never allow real fear to surface. Yet most of us must struggle to make a living, must wonder about our future and about our sense of personal value in a market economy, must deal with the half-articulated and half-understood problems of our children, must fear what our death will be like—what it will mean to die; we must deal with the temptation to believe that life is without meaning, that actions are inconsequential and selfish, and that other people are to be used.

Being a priest does not mean, must not mean, that we are excised from all of that, as if called to deal with others as from a higher eminence; that the struggle for meaning and value and fidelity to the Gospel has been completed in our lives, and that we now deal out of our strengths. God has called us to the salvation of men, and there is no salvation without incarnation. The means of human salvation are other men, as Christ was a man, and we can understand and respond to the degree that we feel ourselves "beset with weakness." If part of our life becomes a subtle, only occasionally noticed effort to maintain a daily sense of priestly call in a culture that increasingly finds us anachronistic and dying—a struggle against a sense of barrenness when God seems so distant, so unreal, and yet his reality is the one thing to which we have given our entire life; an exertion to deal sensitively and honestly with nagging occupations, with difficult colleagues, or with distant superiors in a context that seems lifeless and without promise—then remember that we are called to be men, to enter as Christ so deeply into the human condition that we can redeem it, that our temptations and desolations are the grace of God calling us to a more profound sensitivity with those who are similarly in battle. As we are tempted, as we ourselves suffer or are in pain, so shall we understand the call upon our compassion.

Secondly, weakness more profoundly relates us to God, because it provides the ambit or the arena in which his grace can be seen, in which his sustaining presence can reveal itself, in which even his power can become manifest. This is why it contradicts expectations and stands as almost the contrary of sin. Weakness is the context for the epiphany of the Lord, it is the night in which he appears—not always as felt reassurance, but more often as a power to continue faithful even when we do not feel the strength, even when fidelity means simply putting one foot in front of the other. Paul saw his own life's history as this litany of reversals or sufferings, as linking moments of weakness, but transformed through the supporting power of Christ: "I will all the more gladly boast of my weakness, that the power of God may rest upon me. For the sake of Christ, then, I am content with weaknesses, insults, hardships, persecutions, and calamities; for when I am weak, then I am strong" (2 Corinthians 12:9, 10).

The priest often discovers what his vocation means in these moments, as the power of God becomes evident in the continuity of his life, a fidelity which his weakness would only seem to undermine but actually supports as it evokes the presence of the Lord. Weakness becomes the vocation of the Lord, our call upon him. It is this night, and the heavy work of rowing against the storm, and the threatening waves which brings him to us. It is not that a priest's life would ideally be some other thing—without struggle, self-doubt, or suffering—but that circumstances have unfortunately introduced obdurance and humiliations and a sense of incapacity. Quite the contrary. It is in and through this night that a priest is joined to Christ, as it is in and through this night that he learns that he can trust in the Lord, that he can call out to Jesus in faith, even when this seems the most lifeless thing to do, and find that Jesus Christ is enough. Only in this way will that which we preach and urge upon others become part of our own lives: To commit our lives in trust to the Lord. It is in this experience, the experience of personal weakness, and of having read even limitations as the presence of Christ, of having trusted in him in darkness and having found that one can trust him—it is the experience that joins Christ to his disciples, as he comes to them walking on the waters.

The experience of weakness deepens both our sensitivity to human religious need and our experience in prayer.

There is a collective consequence which follows from all of this. We must make such a life possible for one another. We must support one another in weakness, forgiving one another our daily faults and carrying one another's burdens. It would be absurd to maintain weakness as essentially a part of the priestly vocation and then to belittle those who are deficient; to resent those who are insensitive, unsophisticated, or clumsy; to allow disagreements to become hostilities; or to continue battles and angers because of personal histories. It would be a dreadful thing for us to reject under one criterion or another whom God has called.

The sad fact stands that it is frequently no great trick to get religious men or women to condemn one another. Wars, even personal wars, are terrible realities, and the most horrible of these are religious. For under the guise of good, under the rubric of orthodoxy or liberality, of community or of personal freedom, even of holiness itself, religious men and women can slowly disintegrate into pettiness or cynicism or hostility or bitterness so that "the second state of the man is worse than the first."

Priests are of the same stuff as other men, and they also depend upon men for the unconditioned love of God to be mediated to their weakness. The command of Christ, that we should love one another as he has loved us, is more than a general norm of total benevolence; it is a particular mission: as he cared—out of his weakness—for our weakness, and so became our Eucharist. For us to refuse this support to one another, no matter how religious our articulated standard, is to deceive ourselves almost irremediably and to limit the mercy and understanding of God that should have come through our life. It is not our weakness that hinders the compassion and the goodness of God. It is often what others count our strengths, now become criteria by which we distance ourselves from others not so gifted, interests through which we discover others as boring or unproductive, dedications and religious attainments by which we judge others as mediocre or obviously compromised. There is nothing in our lives that cannot be twisted into a means for evil if we are not discerning, and we know when that moment has come, when Satan has finally effected his transformation into an angel of light, when we have judged others by our own achievements and found them wanting, too inconsequential for our support, unworthy of our time and concern. The greatest protection against this terrible pride—masked as religious seriousness or apostolic commitment, as purity about the things of God, or as honesty about the qualities of men—is an abiding sense of our own weakness, that searing reminder that as we are strengthened by one who has loved us, so we should support one another.

To live this way is to live the paschal mystery of Christ in weakness and in love. We have made a costly choice deciding to become priests, and we should not disguise that choice. Neither should we disguise the love that we are about nor the sense of personal weakness as we confront those lives. God will grace us in the priesthood, in the ministry that lies before us: "He is not weak in dealing with you, but powerful in you. For he was crucified in weakness; but lives by the power of God. For we are weak in Him, but in dealing with you we shall live with him by the power of God" (2 Corinthians 13:3, 4).

PART IV

The Priestly Vocation Today

chapter 15

ON VOCATION

William B. Green

A wise pastor and teacher has written regarding the call to Christian ministry: "There is such a call. . . . I believe with all my heart that a man must hear it and feel its imperious constraint before he can ever give himself with any whole-hearted devotion and abiding wonder to this stewardship of the Gospel. But I believe, too, that more than one minister has been confused by many of the things he has been taught about it and by a great deal that he has read."[1] Recognizing both the necessity of a call and the confusion which it may entail, this essay aims to clarify the idea of vocation as set forth in Scripture, in the Fathers of the Church, the reformers, and subsequent theologians—first as it relates to all believers, then in the narrower sense as it signifies a call to special offices within the Church.

The concept of vocation grew out of Israel's experience of Yahweh as the God who calls. Abraham was called out of his own country, away from kindred and house, and was promised that his descendents were to become the instruments of God's universal, redemptive purpose. Moses received an equally difficult call: to inform Israel in Egypt of Yahweh's intentions, and to be his instrument in bringing Israel out of Egypt.

Without exception, the prophets believed themselves to be called to very specific tasks, in the execution of which they were often isolated from the established religious order. Amos was taken from following the flock and was created and validated a prophet by the word. The call of Yahweh came to Isaiah in the Temple, commissioning him to make his nation stubborn and harden their hearts by the very message he was to proclaim. Jeremiah heard the word empowering him to declare both God's judgment upon his faithless people and his intention to establish a new covenant transformed by mercy. The events leading to the prophets' call were quite diverse, as was also the manner in which the call was received. There were many shades of difference in the prophets' conception of their office. The one constant and indispensable element was the word of Yahweh by which each was claimed for special duties.

But the prophets were not alone in this experience. Israel herself had a divine commission: "I am the Lord, I have called you in righteousness, I have taken you by the hand and kept you; I have given you as a covenant to the people, a light to the nations, . . ."[2]

The notion of call as both an individual and corporate affair is continued in the New Testament. Individuals are summoned to varieties of service in keeping with the diverse gifts of one and the same Spirit. All such gifts are to be used within and for the upbuilding of the body of Christ. In addition, some have been called to specific offices within the Church: "God has appointed in the church first apostles, second prophets, third teachers, . . ."[3] St. Paul claims that the Jewish people still have a special function,[4] while the new Israel, the true sons of Abraham, is thought to be called in the sense of being both summoned and chosen. Especially in Pauline thought, calling and election are substantially the same.[5] Thus there comes to expression with new force the ancient Hebrew conviction that life gains meaning in and through a "calling and direction" by the sovereign word of God. For Christian faith, that word is disclosed with new power and wisdom in Jesus Christ—"at once a promise and an imperative demand for devotion to God and love to fellow men."[6]

As far as the Church Fathers are concerned, the doctrine of vocation is a correlate of the doctrine of creation. Man occupies a special position in the created order as the meeting place of the different spheres of the universe. By virtue of this position, he is to function as cosmic mediator. It is his vocation and task to draw together in himself the material and immaterial, the sensible and intelligible, that through him cosmic harmony may be achieved and deification bestowed upon the whole creation. By nature and calling, man is both priest and king. As priest, he is to sanctify life, bringing it into communion with God, in whom it finds fulfillment. As king, man is given the power to make creation into what God intended it to become. Thus both functions are aspects of a single vocation. The fall of man constituted the rejection of this divine calling.

In Christ, the second Adam, man's original vocation is fulfilled and restored. The one by whom and in whom all things were made in the beginning has renewed and integrated the entire creation by assuming it himself. Christ is, therefore, the one true priest in whose priesthood all who through baptism have been made new are called to participate. He is also the only king through whom man's kingship is re-established. The vocation which man lost as a consequence of the fall is thus restored in Christ who ". . . has made us kings and priests unto God and his Father."[7] As a consequence, man's daily work in all the occupations whereby the fabric of the world is maintained should be verified as having an epiphanic and restorative quality.

A similar understanding of vocation was proclaimed by Martin Luther. Monastic vows rest, according to Luther, on the false assumption that there is a special vocation to which superior Christians are called. But there is no such thing, since the call of God comes to each at his common tasks. In protest against the restriction of vocation to specifically religious jobs, Luther applied the concept to the careers of all Christians. Each person has his own task or station, none of which is to be despised or demeaned. The magistrate has his duty, the minister his, the soldier his, the school teacher his, the physician his, the artist his. One is not better than the other. Each is called to serve God through his daily work. And all Christians are called to be priests one toward another, to act as mediators and intercessors. Everyone must express his faith in loving action designed to bring about a new kind of society, a new quality of life. Thus Luther abolished the distinction between clergy and laity.[8] The doctrine of the universal priesthood of all believers is a consequence of Luther's understanding of baptism. If baptism signifies the return of man to his original role, then it must follow that through baptism his basic vocation with its dual aspects of priesthood and kingship is restored.

While all are priests by virtue of their faith in the word of God, not everyone can or should assume the task of preaching and teaching. Luther argued that for the sake of order, certain persons must be selected to the work and office of the administration of the word of God and the sacraments. "For we must have bishops, pastors or preachers, to give, administer and use, publicly and privately, the four things, or precious possessions, that have been mentioned, for the sake of and in the name of the Church. . . . The whole group cannot do these things, but must commit them, or allow them to be committed, to someone. . . . This duty must be committed to one person, and he alone must be allowed to preach, baptize, absolve, and administer the sacraments. . . ."[9] But, warned Luther, ". . . no one may make use of this power except by the consent of the community or by the call of a superior. For what is the common property of all, no individual may arrogate to himself, unless he be called."[10]

While affirming a universal vocation of priesthood shared by all believers, the Churches of the Anglican tradition recognize that some are called to a specific ministry which is not merely an extension of the common Christian priesthood. The nature of that call originates in and is determined by the special function of the Church itself in relation to

God's reconciling purpose. If the Church is the sacrament of the kingdom of God, then such offices as may exist within the Church must assist
in the realization of that sacramental mission. This means that the
threefold ministry is itself sacramental. It is a gift of the Spirit, a form
of the divine presence. Therefore, no one can take it upon himself to
become a deacon, priest, or bishop. Such vocation can be undertaken
only as a response to the divine initiative and only with the sanction of
duly established authority. One cannot decide on the basis of his own
desires or aptitudes to assume a ministerial office. It is not enough that
one should feel called to such office. The discernment of vocation is by
persistent tradition, a corporate as well as a personal matter. It is the
right and duty of bishops, representing the Church, to select and admit
candidates for holy orders. In the exercise of this responsibility, the
bishop may consult a variety of specialists—physicians, psychiatrists,
psychologists, lay counselors, teachers, priests—as to the state and potential of the applicant. But the decision regarding the ratification of a
vocation is reserved to the bishop.

In his classical statement "On the Unity of the Church," the third-
century bishop, Cyprian, warns against those who attempt to exercise
ecclesiastical office without call and episcopal appointment. "These are
they who, with no appointment from God, take upon them of their own
will to preside over their venturesome companions, establish themselves as rulers without any lawful rite of ordination. These the Holy
Spirit in the Psalms describes as " 'sitting in the seat of pestilence,' a
plague and infection of the faith, deceiving with the mouth of a serpent,
cunning to corrupt truth, vomiting out deadly poisons from pestilential
tongues."[11] Cyprian further argues that the sacraments administered
by these unauthorized persons are ineffective. "While there can be no
Baptism save one only, they think that they can baptize. They forsake
the fountain of life, yet promise the gift of a vital and saving water. Men
are not cleansed by them, but rather made foul; nor their sins purged
away, but even heaped up: it is a birth that gives children not to God,
but to the Devil."[12] As far as Cyprian is concerned, the call to Holy
Orders and the exercise of the same are gifts of grace, not natural rights.
And he foresees only the direst consequences for the Church and its
unity when this is not recognized.

Even Calvin, who did not provide for the office of bishop in the
ecclesiastical structure instituted at Geneva, recognized the need for
corporate confirmation of the individual's call. In the Draft Ecclesiastical Ordinances (1541), he stipulates that ". . . ministers first elect such
as ought to hold offices; afterwards that he be presented to the City
Council; and if he is found worthy the Council receive and accept him,
giving him certification to produce finally to the people when he

preaches, in order that he be received by the common consent of the company of the faithful."[13] Only after this procedure has been observed, is it appropriate "to use the imposition of hands, which ceremony was observed by the apostles and them in the ancient church."

There have been rare instances in which the will of the Church itself constituted the call. One thinks, for example, of Ambrose, who at the time of his election was a Roman magistrate. By his ability to restore order, he so impressed the unruly group assembled to fill the vacant see of Milan that he was unanimously elected bishop. Once the emperor authorized his appointment, Ambrose was baptized, and eight days later consecrated. To Ambrose the election by the assembly was the call of God.

The call to priesthood has as its creative center the proclamation of the word and the administration of the sacraments. Through the communication of the word, apostolic doctrine is preserved and instruction given to the faithful. Through the administration of the sacraments, the most basic of which is the Eucharist, the Church is continually being reconstituted and fulfilled. For the discharge of these functions the priestly office was established and it is to the performance of these tasks that, through the centuries, persons have been called. Together with all members of Christ's Church, the priest is to be a witness to God's concern for the whole creation and for justice and mercy in the affairs of men. In addition, the priest shares with the bishop responsibility for oversight and unity in the Church.

The source and model of this ministry is, of course, Christ himself. He is also the one whose Spirit provides the qualification for such ministry. As St. Paul said: "Before God, we are confident of this through Christ: not that we are qualified in ourselves to claim anything as our own work: all our qualifications come from God. He is the one who has given us the qualifications to be the administrators of this new covenant, which is not a covenant of written letters but of the Spirit: the written letters bring death, but the Spirit gives life."[14]

To declare that the call to and the qualification for priesthood are works of the Spirit is not to remove or deny the personal elements of struggle and growth. Who does not, at some point, doubt whether he has received the call to holy orders? Who is not, from time to time, estranged from the institutional Church and its structures? Who does not wonder whether they can fulfill the demands of priesthood? Who does not know some measure of uncertainty regarding the activity of the Spirit in and through him?

All of these concerns suggest the possibilities for painful struggle, self-doubt, and vocational confusion as well as for development, self-assurance, and spiritual formation, which may be associated with a call to the priesthood. At an even more basic level is the reality of ministry as gift and the experience of that gift.

It is important to note that the gift of ministry, the call to holy orders, does not obliterate human freedom, or deny personal motives, or disregard natural abilities. Grace does not destroy individuality and personhood, but liberates and refines it. Thus, in advising one considering the ministry, account must be taken of the native abilities as well as the skills which a person may have acquired. Is it possible to imagine all of these finding suitable expression in the exercise of the ministry? This is one of the considerations involved in the discernment of vocations.

Concerning those who may require prolonged deliberation before they offer themselves for the priesthood, the former Bishop of Southwell asks: "What valid test or criterion is applicable?" And concludes: "Perhaps the best rough-and-ready answer that can be given, in terms of human judgment, is to say that in all probability a man's vocation is what he can do best, having regard to all relevant circumstances, including his own constitutional make-up, his abilities and disabilities. That may sound mundane and prosaic, pitched in a key too low for so high a theme. But the guidance of God does come through 'circumstances'—the way things are and the way we ourselves are. It is in itself the impact of the Spirit of the living God on the human soul. But we make a mistake if we look for it only in what may seem the more 'spiritual' evidence of exalted emotional experience. . . . And if the decision a man makes is right, if it is in accordance with God's will for him, he ought to be able to justify and defend it by rational and moral arguments without recourse to the language of piety."[15]

This is not to deny the decisive, utterly self-authenticating experience that constitutes for some the call to Christian ministry. But it is to say that such happenings are relatively infrequent. Certainly one should not hold back from offering himself for holy orders just because he lacks that kind of experience.

Statements made earlier regarding one's natural aptitudes for ministry need clarification. That is to say, priesthood is not to be sought either as a resolution of a personal or professional identity problem, or as a means of self-fulfillment or of actualizing one's potential. This is to raise the issue of motives or intentions in offering oneself for holy orders. One may, in fact, discover in the surrender to God's service an identity, a fulfillment as a person which far surpasses one's natural potentialities. As von Balthazar alleges, "The man obedient to his mission fulfills his own being, although he could never find this archetype and ideal of himself by penetrating to the deepest centre of his nature, his super-ego or his subconscious, or by scrutinising his own dispositions, aspirations, talents and potentialities. Simon, the fisherman, before his meeting with Christ, however thoroughly he might have searched within himself, could not possibly have found a trace of Peter. Yet the form 'Peter', the particular mission reserved for him alone, which till then lay hid in the secret of Christ's soul, and at the moment of this encounter, was delivered over to him sternly and imperatively—was to be the fulfillment of all that, in Simon, would have sought vainly for a form ultimately valid in the eyes of God and for eternity. In the form 'Peter' Simon was made capable of understanding the word of Christ, because the form itself issued from the word and was conjoined with it."[16] So the "form" of one's vocation is at one and the same time an act of pure grace, and of one's membership in the Mystical Body of Christ, of having participated wholly in the context of redemption.

Vocation has been spoken of as it applies to all, owing to the restoration of man's nature and place in the universe through Christ's redemptive activity. It is the duty of every man to serve God in whatever work or office he may undertake. Beyond this general vocation shared by all, there are specific offices within the Church to which some are called. This vocation presupposes both a commission to the individual and ratification by the appropriate ecclesiastical authority. There are a number of factors which must be taken into account when deciding whether to pursue holy orders: the individual's aptitudes, motives, and circumstances as well as the Church's evaluation and position. Whatever the outcome, one may be assured that all Christians have a vocation to serve God and to participate in his creative activity.

NOTES

1. Paul Scherer, *For We Have This Treasure* (New York: Harper & Row, 1944), pp. 4–5.

2. Is 42:6; cf. 48:12.

3. 1 Cor 12:27–28.

4. Rom 11:29.

5. Rom 8:28–30; 11:28–29.

6. R. L. Calhoun, in Nelson, J. O., ed. *Work and Vocation in Christian History* (New York: Harper & Row, 1954), pp. 88–89.

7. Rev 1:6.

8. Martin Luther, "The Babylonian Captivity of the Church," *Three Treatises* (Philadelphia: Fortress Press, 1943), p. 234.

9. Quoted in H. T. Kerr, *A Compend of Luther's Theology* (Philadelphia: Westminster Press, 1966), p. 139.

10. Ibid., pp. 137–38.

11. Cyprian, "On the Unity of the Church," chap. X.

12. Cyprian, op. cit.

13. J. K. S. Reid, ed. and trans., *Calvin: Theological Treatises,* Library of Christian Classics, vol. 22 (Philadelphia: Westminster Press, 1953), p. 59.

14. 2 Cor 3:4–6.

15. F. R. Barry, *Vocation and Ministry* (London: J. Nisbet, 1958), p. 22.

16. H. U. von Balthazar, *Prayer* (New York: Sheed & Ward, Inc., 1967), p. 49.

chapter 16

PRIESTHOOD AND THE CHURCH AS COMMUNITY

Arthur A. Vogel

As the twentieth century reached its midpoint, prominent theologians were prophesying that future ages would look back on our epoch as the "Century of the Church."

As this century progresses, there are increasing indications that the prophecy may prove to be true. Aided by the insights of Vatican II, a new appreciation of the life of early Christians, and the admission that the fragmentation of the Church dishonors the oneness of Christ, we are growing in our understanding of the nature and vocation of the Church. Above all, the Church is increasingly recognized to be much more than a formal institution; it is a people called by God, a community of witness.

The Spirit seems again to be mysteriously moving in the Church, and the renewal resulting from that movement is also playing an important role in the rediscovery of the Church's nature. One of the acknowledged promptings of the Spirit is to replace thoughts of "I" by thoughts of "we." The Spirit of Christ is the Spirit of humility and reconciliation. It is the Spirit who guides us to understand the Christian life in terms of fellowship, celebration, interdependence, and mutuality.

Growth in understanding the Church as a eucharistic fellowship, that is, as a community *constituted* and *structured* by the Eucharist—not just as a group of people who occasionally do the Eucharist among other things—is also leading to a reappraisal of the Church. The Eucharist epitomizes Christian community, for the Eucharist is an action involving community in its totality. In the divine liturgy, a person appointed by ordination presides at an assembly of people, but the recalling ordered by Christ for his people is made by the assembly as a whole, each person having his or her own liturgy to perform in a way compliment-

141

ing rather than replacing others. Such complimentarity is the only way members of Christ's mystical body can be related to each other in the sacramental body, and such interdependence and complimentarity must be evident in all truly Christian authority, mission, and ministry.

The Church is a community of faith, the Mystical Body of Christ, whose purpose is to reconcile the world to God in the power of the resurrection. "All ministries are used by the Holy Spirit for the building up of the Church to be this reconciling ministry for the glory of God and the salvation of men (Ephesians 4:11–13)."[1] But because ministries inspired by the Spirit within the Church are so diverse, a need was felt even in New Testament times to focus and promote communal unity: the community's diverse activities needed to be coordinated; the mission of the Church needed to be ordered; and the movements of the Spirit needed discernment. The episcopacy developed to perform those services. The Church's understanding of the nature of ordination and of the role of the ordained ministry in the life of the Church were developed from these beginnings.

The Church as a whole has a ministry in the world to the world, and the ordained, particular ministry has as its purpose the enabling of that universal ministry. The same thing may be said in terms of priesthood: there is a universal priesthood of the Church in which every Christian participates by virtue of his baptism; that priesthood is coextensive with the membership and purpose of the Church as a whole, and is the priesthood referred to in 1 Peter 2:9 when Christians are said to be "a chosen race, a royal priesthood, a holy nation, God's own people, . . ." The ordained, particular priesthood exists to enable the universal priesthood to be itself. The ordained priesthood always exists within the Church for the Church.

Having briefly observed the origins of episcopacy, we should notice the origin of the other orders of ministry as they developed in the earliest period of the Church's life. As the person expressing the Church's unity and exercising oversight in the community, it was the bishop who presided at the eucharistic assembly in the early Church; he, insofar as he was chief servant of the community and bearer of its tradition—not as an individual in his own right—also had the ability to ordain others for the service of the Church.

In the next development, accordingly, we find bishops associating other persons with them and their activities by means of ordination. Priests or "presbyters are joined with the bishop in his oversight of the Church and in the ministry of the word and sacraments; they are given authority to preside at the eucharist and to pronounce absolution. Deacons, although not so empowered, are associated with bishops and presbyters in the ministry of word and sacrament, and assist in oversight."[2]

By means of ordination a person enters a new community within the larger Christian community, a ministerial community. One type of such community includes the bishop and the presbyters; another type includes the bishop and deacons. Through the laying on of hands at ordination, a special gift of the Spirit is given to the one ordained, but because ordination is also in and for the whole community of the Church, ordinations duly performed, are the means by which the Church is able to recognize and assure itself that those who claim to be its servants actually have received the grace God intends for such service. As with every sacramental rite, ordination is intended to be the means by which the Church is assured that what God promises to his Church has in fact been given to those who need it.

In considerations such as those we are presently undertaking, it is very important that, in our search for clarity and ease of understanding, we do not reduce the Church as the living, Mystical Body of Christ to something less than itself. The Church is the unique presence of God in the world and as such has many dimensions. It has recently been pointed out that we must use a number of models in our attempt to understand the nature of the church.[3] A difficulty encountered is that the models which must be employed for our understanding are not to be used one at a time; they must all be held in tension at the same time. No one can deny, for example, that the Church is an institution in the world; that it is one model, complete with administrators, leaders, and followers. But the Church is also and more importantly a herald, a servant, a community, and a sacrament. Different features of the Church are emphasized by each model, but no model can properly obliterate those dimensions of the Church presented by the other models.

Considering the nature of ordination and the role of the ordained ministry in the Church, however, few will deny that western Christendom has for many centuries seen an overemphasis of the "power" of the clergy as rulers of the Church at the expense of the Church as a community. Ordination does bestow a special gift of the Spirit, but for too long that gift was exercised as a personal power which the clergy used for and over the rest of the people of God. It has even been suggested by one theologian that "the minister's representative relation to Christ, as his ambassador, is in every way prior to his relation to the Church, as its liturgical agent."[4] Such an overemphasis of ministerial power denies the fact that ministry of any order is always of the Church, for the Church, and within the Church. The ordained ministry exists within community, for community, as does every sacrament. The point is that the "power" of ministry cannot be isolated from its place in community for even an instant. Christian community and power are correlatives;

that is, each term in the pair necessarily refers to the other in order to be itself.

It has been said by a group of Anglican theologians that the Anglican Church, from the time of the Reformation, has tried to bear witness to the principle "that one who exercises authority and who has certain powers within a community is not above those whom he serves. Authority and power have meaning and validity only as they are exercised within the Body and for the Body. In practice this principle meant, and still means to this day, that no Bishop has the authority or the power, simply by right of his consecration, to act without the consent of the community of which he is a servant. . . . A Bishop's power is not his own. . . ."[5]

It was from such considerations as these that the House of Bishops, meeting in Chicago, declared that "the necessary conditions for valid ordination to the Priesthood in the Episcopal Church were not fulfilled on the occasion [of the July 29, 1974, service of ordination in Philadelphia]. . . ."

As might be expected from the conditions under which the bishops were forced to meet and deliberate, all dimensions of the problem confronting the Church could not be explored during the meeting; thus the possibilities of misinterpreting the bishops' intention were many. The use of the concept of validity, for example, has led to an especially unfortunate overreaction on the part of some to the claimed "invalidity" of the Philadelphia service. The overreaction of even trained theologians perhaps shows how sensitive Anglicans still are to the papal declaration on the invalidity of Anglican orders as being "absolutely null and utterly void." So it was that the theological committee of the House of Bishops, meeting in Oaxtapec, Mexico, clarified its use of the term "valid." The committee stated:

When a sacrament is said to be valid we understand "validity" to mean that the sacramental action is "assured," that its efficacy is "certain." Such assurance and certainty are not found in the Philadelphia service according to this House, and we agree. . . . No merely minor irregularity was involved. . . .

In itself, the term "irregularity" can refer to both insignificant and grave departures from a norm. The sacraments are meant to be signs of certitude for the Church that what God has promised to his Church has been duly offered on a given occasion. Minor irregularities in sacramental administrations do not destroy the certitude of which we are speaking, but a degree of irregularity can be found which casts public doubt on what is meant to be the means of public certitude. It was the latter degree of irregularity the House of Bishops found lacking in the

Philadelphia service. The House was trying to stress the gravity of the irregularity; the irregularity was not just a canonical, legalistic nicety. It affected the essential nature of the ordained ministry and its place in the community it serves.

As I have stated, keeping the proper balance between different tensions is always difficult, but for a Christian such balance is absolutely necessary when considering the nature of the Church. The Church as the Mystical Body of Christ is not a machine; God did not start it going and then abandon it to impersonal laws or human powers. Life in the Church is the constant confrontation with, and participation in, mystery. In fact, every fully theological judgment is a moral judgment because it involves the relation of persons to each other and to God.

As we morally relate to other people and to God, no factor in a situation can safely be put aside as unimportant. That is the reason we are counseled not to judge one another in this life; God is the only judge, for he is the only one who knows the secrets of the heart. From the point of view of our principles, we sometimes condemn the behavior of others, but we must remember that principles are abstract while people are not. For these reasons, no sacramental judgment made for the good order and identity of the Church should ever be taken as an ultimate, moral judgment of another person. That is true even of such an extreme judgment as excommunication.

All of that having been said, however, criteria for certitude at the level of community life are necessary if the Church, as a community in the world, is to have an identity distinct from other communities. For Christians, sacraments are the divinely appointed means of communal identity and certitude. If such certitude were not appointed for the Church, the Church would be no more than an agglomeration of individuals and private opinions. That is the view some people have of the Church, of course, but if that contention is correct, the Church is not the Spirit-filled body of Christ.

In sacramental action the Church uniquely acts *as a Church*, for the sacraments are gifts of God to his people as a whole. The sacraments do not belong to individuals or dioceses. Where the communal structure, process, and nature of the Church are appropriated by individuals for themselves, certain members of the body try to act as if they were the whole body. In such action the Church is not compelled to say that the *Church's* will has been done.

That is especially true of the sacrament of ordination, for in it the Church commissions, by means of God's grace, its own servants. There is a certain equivocation between "the Church" and "the Churches" today because of the fragmentation of the body of Christ by human sin, but as faithful followers of Christ we must always try to act in the largest consensus possible within the Church. That is how we witness at the same time to the oneness of Christ and to the universality of the Church; such witness is vitally important where the very structure of the Church—the sacraments—is concerned.

When the common practice and understanding of the Catholic Church—or of a given Church—are radically altered by a proposed sacramental change, obviously specific individuals cannot usurp the role of the Church as a whole in the latter's universal and communal aspects. To ordain women to the priesthood and episcopacy is such a change in the common practice and understanding of the catholic Church. I personally believe the change can be made, but I do not believe that our present knowledge precludes the possibility of our being wrong on either side of the issue. If the change is to be made, then, a chance is being taken, and it must be taken by no less an agent than a Church acting in its communal integrity, for ordination is meant to be a sign of the Church's communal integrity.

Only the Church as an ecclesial community, by means of its own communal processes, can determine and recognize who will be its servants. Ordination is not anyone's right, let alone a civil right, and the Church is not a secular society whose elements are of human determination alone. Those are the truths becoming most obscured in the present controversy.

NOTES

1. *Ministry and Ordination: A Statement on the Doctrine of the Ministry Agreed by the Anglican-Roman Catholic International Commission,* Canterbury 1973 (London: S.P.C.K., 1973), no. 5.

2. Ibid., no. 9.

3. Avery Dulles, *Models of the Church* (Garden City: Doubleday & Co., 1974), *passim.*

4. Michael Bruce and G. E. Duffield, eds. *Why Not? Priesthood and the Ministry of Women* (Appleford, Abingdon, Berkshire: Marcham Books, 1972), p. 80.

5. Statement of the faculty of Nashotah House Theological Seminary, July 22, 1975.

chapter 17

PRIESTLY CHARACTER

John Macquarrie

We live in the age of functional man. That is to say, a man or woman is considered in terms of what he or she does. A man, for example, is a train driver or a bank clerk. Of course, no one is a driver or a clerk all the time. But then we speak of roles, and this too is a functional term. When the bank clerk comes home at night, he lays aside his working role and takes up the roles of husband and father. What we seem afraid to do is ever to come to the person himself, the person who in some sense remains identical through the many roles and functions, the person who not only *does* things but *is* someone. Perhaps indeed we have come to doubt whether there is a personal reality, for in the depersonalized world of today we act much of the time as if people were nothing but the sums or aggregates of changing functions and roles. Gabriel Marcel has said that one of the diseases of our time is the loss of the ontological sense. Man has become so absorbed in what he does that he no longer has any sense of who he is.

There is, of course, some truth in the idea of functional man. It is through our deeds and decisions that we become persons, and what we do makes us who we are. But the human reality is not exhausted by the functions which any individual performs.

Surely the Christian minister in particular is more than his functions. We can list his various roles and functions—he is servant, proclaimer, priest; he preaches, baptizes, presides at the Eucharist; he does many things besides. But it makes sense to ask: *Who* is it that appears in these roles and performs these functions? Daniel Day Williams made the essential point when he wrote: "Vocation is more than a role; it is a life dedicated and a responsibility assumed. No one should be playing a role at the point where ultimate things are at stake."[1]

If ministry were merely a role or a collection of functions, then there might seem to be no need for a distinctive ordained ministry in the

147

Church, and this idea has an appeal in our egalitarian age. The Church
would consist, so to speak, of modular Christians, any one of whom
might be fitted into the appropriate functional slot. Certainly, everyone
recognizes that some functions need training and preparation and that
not everyone could get up and preach. But is presidency at the Eucharist, for instance, merely performing the function of reciting certain
words and doing certain acts, so that any Christian who is literate and
has had a little practice could do this as well as anyone else? Or is there
more to it? Is there a deeper connection between ministry and presiding at the Eucharist than can be expressed by terms like "role" and
"function"? Or again, can this particular function be separated and
considered in isolation from that whole constellation of functions which
constitute the work of an ordained minister?

I think there is much more to ministry and priesthood than the
fulfilling of roles and functions. R. C. Moberly expressed the matter
thus:

There are not only priestly functions or priestly prerogatives; there is also a
priestly spirit and a priestly heart—more vital to the true reality of priesthood
than any mere performance of priestly functions. Now this priestly spirit is not
the exclusive possession of the ordained ministry; it is the spirit of the priestly
Church. But those who are ordained 'priests' are bound to be eminently leaders
and representatives of this priestliness of spirit, and they have assigned to them
an external sphere and professional duties which constitute a special opportunity, and a charisma of grace which constitutes a special call and a special
capacity for its exercise. Such opportunity and call are inseparable from the
oversight of the Christian community to Godward, and they are as wide as is
the life of the Christian body. Leadership in eucharistic worship, truly understood, is its highest typical expression . . . but eucharistic leadership, truly
understood, involves many corollaries of spirit and life.[2]

It is not meant that the ordained minister is somehow better or more
inward or more spiritual than his lay brothers and sisters. But within the
order and economy of the Church he is distinct, for he has received a
special call, accepted a special responsibility, and been given in ordination a special grace to strengthen him. When we remember that ministry is a grace or gift bestowed by Christ, we shall not be in danger of
thinking that the ordained ministry is a superior caste in the Church.
The ordained ministry owes everything to Christ—it is indeed Christ's
ministry embodied in a certain way. This is recognized by the Church's
teaching that the validity of a sacrament does not depend on the personal worthiness of the priest. Christ himself is the true minister of
every sacrament, and the unworthiness of the human agent cannot void
Christ's bestowal of grace. Of course, this was never intended to suggest

that the minister's worthiness or unworthiness is a matter of indifference! Effectual priesthood demands not just the *doing* of the priestly act but *being* a priest in union with the great high priest, Jesus Christ.

The traditional word used by theologians to designate the peculiar being or status of the ordained priest, that which underlies and unites his various roles and functions and finds expression in them, is the word "character." This is not a popular word at the present time. To those whose minds are pragmatic, empirical, analytic, the idea of character may seem just a mystification. They feel safer in dealing with functional man.

Now I do not deny that the traditional doctrine of a priestly character was often described in categories which nowadays we judge to have been too metaphysical and impersonal for describing the kind of phenomenon which is here in question. To some extent, this may excuse the impatience with the idea of character found in some modern writers on ministry. Anthony Harvey, for instance, brusquely dismisses the idea of character as something that "can find no place" in his account of ministry.[3] But it cannot be so quickly dismissed, nor is a merely functional approach adequate in the least. The contemporary theologian has got to find more up-to-date and personal categories in which to express the abiding truth in the idea of priestly character.

In its literal sense, the Greek word *charakter* signified the distinctive mark made by a seal or die or similar instrument. The word is used only once in the New Testament, in the Epistle to the Hebrews, where Jesus Christ is said to be "the express image of God's person" or, alternatively translated, "the very stamp of his nature" (Hebrews 1:3). In modern usage, the word "character" has developed a great many meanings, but for our purpose we shall take our clues mainly from ethical usage, for there is a close parallel between the ethical idea of character and the theological idea.

The parallel emerges right away, because just as we have seen that there are two views of the ministry standing in some tension, the functional view concerned primarily with what the minister does and the ontological view concerned with who he is, so there have long been two types of ethical theory, the one understanding morality chiefly in terms of rules, commandments, acts, overt behavior, the other understanding the moral life more in terms of virtue and the formation of moral persons or even communities. It is no accident that the morality of command and act has, in the specific area of Christian ethics, flourished chiefly among Protestants, while Catholic moral theologians have been preoccupied with the ethics of virtue. Likewise, many Protestant theologians tend to view ministry in a functional way, while such ideas as priestly character and formation have dominated Catholic thinking.

But although the two approaches have often been in tension, my own view is that in both ethics and theology they are finally complementary. The merely functional approach is superficial and fails to do justice to the personal reality, but it is not canceled out by the ontological understanding of the matter; rather, it is given depth and cohesion.

How then does a modern ethicist think of character? Clearly, character is not a thing or a special faculty. It is more like a pattern, traceable in a person's behavior and showing elements of directionality and consistency. Stanley Hauerwas, author of one of the best recent studies of the subject, writes: "The clearest example of character is one in which a life is dominated by one all-consuming purpose or direction."[4] This would be an extreme case, and there can be strong characters where there are many purposes and interests, provided these are brought into unity by an "ultimate concern" (to borrow Tillich's useful expression) giving, as it were, a recognizable set to the agent's policies.

But although character is a pattern discernible in action and built up in action, it is not just an adjective or product of action. On the contrary, character produces some actions rather than others, for it is constituted by the value judgments and priorities of the agent, and is hardly to be distinguished from the agent himself.

It is clear that character cannot be acquired in a moment. It needs formation, and that may take a long time. Once character has been formed, it introduces a pattern of stability and reliability into life, but this does not mean an end to growth. Character deepens and develops in the face of new problems.

Where does character come from? Obviously it has several sources. There is the given genetic inheritance of every individual, his innate propensities, capacities, weaknesses. This is the raw material of character. Within limits, it determines what it is possible for one to become. But this raw material is plastic and has many possibilities inherent in it. Next, there is everything that happens to a person from outside. There are the accidents of his own history, and these may have good or bad influence. There is the impact of his culture, and none of us can help absorbing many of the beliefs and value judgments of contemporary society. There is the important factor of education, the systematic training of mind and spirit. These three influences that come from outside we may call the passive elements in character formation. But there is also an active factor. To some extent, each one of us chooses to be the kind of person that he or she is. We strive to realize an ideal self of our own choosing. Finally, to the factors already mentioned, the Christian would add divine grace. He believes that the attainment of character is not just an accident of birth or environment or the fruit of unaided human struggle, but that prayer, the sacraments, and life in the Christian community are of supreme importance.

The foregoing discussion relates to character in general from the standpoint of ethical theory. What light does it throw on the theological concept of priestly character? We shall answer this question by considering the steps by which one enters the ordained ministry. These can be understood as steps in the formation of special types of character.

First there is vocation, the calling of God. Priesthood is a gift, it is not something we choose for ourselves. When a priest is asked: "What made you decide to enter the ministry?" he may very likely reply that he hardly knows. He may only be able to say that at some time he felt a calling. The call to the ministry is a special case or an extension of the mystery of election, which all Christians have known to some extent. It is that inner constraint, that claim of God, that fascination with Christ which lays hold upon one and draws one on, perhaps at first unwillingly. The call to the ministry is an extension of election, the summons to a new relationship. Already the experience of this calling has its ontological consequence and has begun to shape the character of the one who is called; for no one who has known such a call can ever be quite the same again.

Next, God's call elicits the human response. Character is formed not only by what comes from outside but by our own active pursuit of an ideal, and this is true of priestly character. It requires the dedication and self-giving of the one who is called. We have seen that character is formed when one is devoted to an "ultimate concern." The coming of God's kingdom in the world, and the service of that kingdom, become the focal interest of the Christian minister and give the distinctive set to his character. There is also the negative side. To choose one thing means to renounce other things. The ordination vows speak not only of what is to be chosen and done, but also of "laying aside the study of the world and the flesh." Sacrifice is a necessary element in the priestly character. In consenting to become this kind of person and to let his character be formed around the focus of serving God's kingdom, the priest must make renunciations.

I think there are different permissible interpretations of what this focusing and its accompanying renunciations will mean in priesthood. The Church will always need some whose intense dedication will lead them to celibacy and the severing of all ties that might seem to them to be obstacles to their vocation. Others believe that the priestly character can be formed in lives that are more diversified and cover a broader segment of human interests, including marriage and the family. Still others—and perhaps an increasing number—will combine priesthood with a secular occupation. I believe that all these styles are possible, provided always that there is that fundamental orientation toward the calling of God, the orientation that is a major factor in the formation of the priestly character.

Priesthood is a lifelong vocation and a lifelong commitment, and indeed it takes a lifetime for the full flowering of priestly character. The formation of this character becomes an irreversible process, and this is what is meant by the traditional language about the "indelibility" of the character. But we live nowadays in a time when many are unwilling to make lifelong commitments, whether in vocation or marriage or other ways. Should there then be temporary ordinations? This question must be answered in the negative. A temporary priesthood would be conceivable only on a purely functional view; it is impossible on the deeper conception which I am trying to expound. But what is possible is a temporary commitment to particular forms or styles of ministry. I said the Church will always need some ministers who will dedicate themselves with an exclusive intensity that eschews all worldly ties. Surely there are in the Church today young priests who might be willing to promise that for five years they would not marry, they would live on a minimal wage, they would serve wherever the Church needed them. Such a corps of utterly dedicated young priests could become the shock troops of the Church and might accomplish much in evangelism and renewal.

Vocation and response do not happen just between an individual and God, but in the context of the Church, which tests the calling of the individual, judges his fitness, and provides the training he needs. It is this period of formation that is of vital importance in the making of a priest, and though priestly character is ontological, it is in no sense magical. This is no place to raise the vast questions relating to the training of ministers, but whatever else is done, it is essential that there should be formed a character marked by devotion to God and his kingdom, openness and responsiveness to others, and inward strength of spirit.

I have still to mention something else. Vocation, response, formation in the Church culminate in ordination, with its gift of sacramental grace. God commits himself to his ministers, and this is more important than their commitment to what is, from the human point of view, an impossible vocation. Priests sin like other human beings, but God keeps recalling them, electing them again to be his representatives in the assembly of his people. And this process goes on in the years after ordination. Character does not fall ready-made from heaven at ordination or any other time, but it deepens through this life and beyond.

I have stressed priestly character as a distinctive gift for those who are called to a distinctive ministry, but finally I want to come back to the point that all this happens in the context of the Church. The distinctive ministries are closely related with the general ministry of the whole Church. Thus we have seen that calling to the priesthood has affinity with the mystery of election that touches every Christian, and we could also say that priestly character is a special development of the character which originates in baptism. The general ministry of the Church and the distinctive ordained ministry are closely related because they are both modes of sharing in the ministry of Christ himself, but they are different modes of sharing. There is distinction without separation within the indivisible body of the Church, which will be all the stronger and better equipped for its mission if we are careful neither to break up what is common to all ministry nor to blur what is distinctive. For this ministry is Christ's gift to his Church for the sanctifying of his people and, indeed, of the whole creation, that he may present it blameless to the Father.

NOTES

1. D. D. Williams, *The Minister and the Care of Souls* (New York: Harper & Row, 1961), p. 103.

2. R. C. Moberly, *Ministerial Priesthood* (London: John Murray, 1910), p. 261.

3. A. E. Harvey, *Priest or President?* (London: Darton, Longman, and Todd, 1975), pp. 49–50.

4. S. Hauerwas, *Character and the Christian Life* (San Antonio, Texas: Trinity University Press, 1975), p. 119.

chapter 18

THE BIBLE, THE NATURE OF THE CHURCH AND THE ORDINATION OF WOMEN

Harvey H. Guthrie, Jr.

It is my conviction that the biblical understanding of the nature of the Church not only presents no obstacle to the ordination of women to the priesthood and the episcopate, but that the very nature of God's *ekklesia* ("Church"), as it is understood in the Scriptures of both the old Israel and the new, *requires* the opening of ordination to women, once the question has been raised. That conviction is based on my understanding of what "Israel" really means in the Old Testament and of what *ekklesia* really means in the New Testament.

ISRAEL IN THE OLD TESTAMENT

There runs through the Bible a basic contrast, the contrast between Israel as the people of God and the *goyim.* To understand that contrast, as it has so often been understood, as between an "in group" over against unworthy outsiders—Gentiles or pagans—is to misread it. The contrast between "Israel" and *goyim* is much deeper, much more radical, much better news than that to finite human beings.

Goy is what any human being is in terms of where and when and into what race and nation and class and sex one was born. What *goy* one is, is justified in terms of a cosmic myth. That was true in the ancient Middle Eastern world of Israel, in the Mediterranean world of the Roman Empire and the early Church, and even in the modern world of secularism and bicentennial national celebrations. The cosmic myth always indicates how the divine order ordains and validates the status, the *goy*ness, human beings live in, in terms of their place and race and nation and class and sex.

155

There are two recurring difficulties with that world view. The first is that there are numerous varieties of *goy*ness: Babylonian versus Assyrian, Roman versus Barbarian, American versus Russian, white versus black, and so on. When two such varieties of *goy*ness encounter one another—each justified as normative by a cosmic myth—logic requires the conquest of one or the other by one or the other. How, after all, could the divine order ordain more than one *goy?* That question is the reason for the conquest and war by which *goy* history has always been characterized. Ancient "wise men," like the writer of the Tower of Babel story in Genesis, and the author of Ecclesiastes; and modern "wise men," like Mark Twain, have been more perceptive about that than have *goy* folk living inside cosmic myths.

The second difficulty with this classically pervasive world view is that it always underwrites the "outsideness" and the oppression of people like slaves and Gypsies and Indians and immigrants. It cannot be affirmative about the differentness of peoples who push in from the desert, who are captured and imported as slaves, or who immigrate into the established social order. The only alternative for such peoples in relation to a *goy* order, if they wish to "make it," is to infiltrate the order or to take it over by force, and then find justification for themselves in terms of the cosmic myth. That is why, and cynical "wise men" have seen this too, history is so largely the record of those who have conquered *goy* orders at the price of losing their own distinctive identity as human beings.

Israel originated in the ancient Middle Eastern world as a people called away from the *goy* world by a God whose vitality defied the recurrent repetition of the cosmic myth, and required the recital of a series of unique events in which that God demonstrated that the ultimate power of the universe did not justify any one *goy* order over against any other, and did not validate the exclusion or oppression of any class or people. Israel was, by definition, no *goy*. Israel was a league of different tribes. Israel was a confederation of different *goyim*, the *qahal* or "congregation" of that God. Membership in Israel was open in theory to whoever "feared" that God and entered into covenant with that God.

Israel's normative self-understanding is expressed in the account of Abraham's origins in Genesis 11 and 12. There it is stated that the history of salvation began precisely when Abraham turned his back on the genealogy that connected him with the great *goy* enterprise described in the Tower of Babel story. Israel came into being in response to a call from God which, if responded to, led to a new kind of identity and *raison d'être* in which there was blessing for every different human family of *goyim*. In line with that, the continual theme of Israel's prophets, in successively unique historical situations, was a calling of Israel from *goy* self-preservation to that inclusive "peopleness" which was Israel's essential nature under God. Israel was not a *goy*, an ethnic or national religious community in which some one brand of humanness was underwritten by a cosmic myth. Israel was a people called into being across *goy* lines by a good God whose goodness saw every last different brand of humanness as good, and whose purpose would be fully accomplished only when Exodus freedom was enjoyed by every last human tribe in free covenant with that God.

Israel was, however, certainly culturally and socially and politically and psychologically a part of the human world in which Israel lived. That world took kingship and patriarchy and slavery for granted. Yet the logic of what Israel essentially was worked itself out in remarkable ways, given Israel's environment. No Israelite king was ever able to be a king in the absolute *goy* sense. The regulations regarding slaves in Israel's law incorporate a humane attitude that was ultimately to undermine slavery as an institution. The patriarchal assumptions that women are property do prevail in specific regulations and with regard to the role of women in the "congregation." The logic of what Israel essentially was, however, works itself out in such a way that monogamy comes to be taken for granted, in spite of what the ancient laws say.

Finally, for our purposes, the carefully worked out theological prelude to Israel's Scriptures in Genesis 1 sums all that up with regard to the status of women by denying what is implicit in Genesis 2 and 3, the section so often quoted in support of the subservience of women. Genesis 1 includes female as well as male in the category *'adam*, or "humanity." The logic of the nature of Israel was working itself out in the perception of the priestly writer of Genesis 1 in a way that was directly contrary to a lot of culturally conditioned, traditional material preserved on succeeding pages. Something was being said that demanded finally being witnessed to in an Israel that was really transcending *goy*ness and living as the people of God.

"CHURCH" IN THE NEW TESTAMENT

When we turn from the Old Testament to the New, we find that that body of people in the Roman Empire, which found itself existing as a result of the life and death and resurrection of Jesus of Nazareth, understood itself in the same way as had ancient Israel. They believed that precisely the same God was at work in a new and unique way to form an inclusive people out of the variety of *goy*nesses to be found in the Roman Empire. When they tried to understand what was happening in them and among them, they found the clue in the recorded experience of the ancient people from which some of them had come—in the Hebrew Scriptures. They could describe themselves only as a new *Israel*, as the *ekklesia* (the Greek for *qahal*) or Church of God, as a people gathered from many *ethnai* (the Greek for *goy* and the origin of "ethnic").

There are, of course, many places in the New Testament which, like many places in the Old Testament, mirror the cultural and sociological and political attitudes of the time. When, however, New Testament writers are driven directly to face the implications, for a given situation, of the essential nature of the Church, as *ekklesia* of God over against human ethnicity, the biblical logic comes through. When, for example, St. Paul, or someone writing in his name, is more concerned about the Church's public relations than its essential nature, he exhorts people to abstain from buying meat offered symbolically to idols, even though it does not mean a thing; or exhorts slaves to be submissive to their masters, even though God's sovereignty takes precedence over all other; or exhorts women to cover their heads in public, to remain quiet in public, and to conform to the accepted marital mores. When, however, St. Paul is addressing himself to the essential nature of the Church as that nature relates to some specific issue, the basic logic comes out: "All baptized in Christ, you have all clothed yourselves in Christ, and there are no more distinctions between Jew and Greek, slave and free, male and female, but all of you are one in Christ Jesus" (Galatians 3:27–28).

THE NATURE OF THE CHURCH AND THE "JUDAIZING" CONTROVERSY

In the course of its history the Church has had to deal with three crucial confrontations about the logic of its nature. Interestingly, the content of those three confrontations follows successively the three areas of unity mentioned by St. Paul in the verses quoted just above.

The first confrontation occurred in the New Testament period, and is the one to which St. Paul is really addressing himself in those verses. It was the so-called Judaizing controversy. Because the earliest Christians were Jews, and because the Church's understanding of itself was so firmly based on ancient Israel's self-understanding, it came to be asserted that to be a Christian one had first to be a Jew, and then to continue in the practice of all the precepts of Judaism in order to continue being a Christian. Apparently that position was held by Gentile converts in some cases as enthusiastically as by Jews.

St. Paul perceived that to be a direct challenge to the essential nature of the Church. He saw it, in the situation obtaining in his time, to be a reduction of the *ekklesia* of God to ethnicism, just as the ancient prophets had seen Israel's reactions to certain ancient situations as a reduction of Israel to *goy*ness. St. Paul perceived the position of the Judaizers to be a human betrayal of the purpose God had in mind when God began that biblical, incarnational initiative in the call to Abraham. That is why those lines about there being no distinction between Jew and Greek (that is what St. Paul was emphasizing), slave and free, male and female, are followed by, "Merely by belonging to Christ you are already the posterity of Abraham, the heirs he was promised" (Galatians 3:29).

To those who were quoting the Scriptures and invoking the divine law in support of the Judaizing position, St. Paul's words were absurdly and blasphemously radical. St. Paul, however, perceived that the essential nature of the Church, precisely as the new Israel, required such words, and required as well not only the baptism of Gentiles, but the inclusion of Gentiles in his own apostolic ministry. Only so could that ministry embody what was true of the essential nature of the Church. We now take the Pauline position on Judaizing for granted, but its logic leads the Church further.

THE NATURE OF THE CHURCH AND THE INSTITUTION OF SLAVERY

The second crucial confrontation about the logic of the nature of the Church took place centuries after the New Testament period. It had to do with the institution of slavery, and, we have only now begun to see, with the racism involved—given the race of those who were slaves in Western society. The issue was raised by some within the Church, but it was raised by those outside the Church as well. The latter should be remembered, given what is being said about the advocacy of the ordination of women being interference in the Church's affairs by a feminist movement that is secular and humanist.

Arguments justifying slavery were advanced from Scripture and tradition and divine law, just as they had been advanced for the Judaizing position. Here is a description of the position of an eminent American Anglican bishop, Dr. Samuel Seabury of New York, written just before the Civil War under the title, *American Slavery Distinguished from the Slavery of English Theorists and Justified by the Law of Nature:*

In his Preface he deplores the fact that the question of slavery should "be complicated with questions of morality, religion, and social reputation." He makes a determined effort to distinguish true slavery as condemned in England and elsewhere from the beneficent institution found in the South. Its supporters in America, he maintains, stand for order, conservatism, and Christianity; whereas its opponents are too often identified with anarchy and infidelity. The slaves must be presumed to have consented to their status, and their relation to their masters is now established by the decree of divine Providence. Not only is slavery not forbidden by the New Testament, but "the precepts of love and equity enjoined on us by our Blessed Lord have no such tendency as is supposed to impair and ultimately subvert the relation of master and slave." (J. T. Addison, *The Episcopal Church in the U.S. 1789–1931*, p. 194)

A probably apocryphal story about Abraham Lincoln, however, indicates a different view of Scripture and tradition and divine law. On the eve of the 1860 election, Lincoln was checking the estimate of how his home town would vote. When he expressed particular interest in the clergy, and was shown the results, Lincoln is reported to have said: "Here are twenty-three ministers of different denominations, and all of them are against me but three; and here are a great many prominent members of churches, a very large majority of whom are against me." Then, with tears in his eyes, he continued, "I know there is a God, and that He hates injustice and slavery. I see the storm coming, and I know that His hand is in it. If He has a place and work for me I believe I am ready. I am nothing but truth is everything." He then went into a "lengthy and dark meditation" on God and Christ, slavery and the teachings of the New Testament, and concluded, "I may not see the end, but it will come, and I shall be vindicated; and these men will find they have not read their Bibles aright." (Carl Sandburg, *The Prairie Years*, II, 372–373)

The issue before the Church in connection with slavery in the nineteenth century, like the issue in the Judaizing controversy of the first century, had to do with the nature of the Church as *ekklesia* of God, as new Israel. Lincoln perceived the biblical logic correctly. We now recognize what the real issue was, even though we have not followed through on all the consequences of it—not even in the Boston area where I am writing this! We now know that, well-intentioned as he was, Bishop Seabury, in his concern for order and his invocation of Providence and the law of nature, was missing the real issue. We recognize too that the ordained ministry which is representative of the Church must embody those races excluded from it by Seabury's logic if God's logic for his trans-*goy* people is to be expressed. We have done that by including a celebration of the ministry of Absalom Jones in the calendar of the Episcopal Church.

What was at stake for the Church in the 1860s in connection with the question of slavery was the very nature of the Church as Church. We now take Lincoln's position on slavery for granted, just as we take St.

Paul's on Judaizing for granted, but its logic leads the Church still further.

THE NATURE OF THE CHURCH
AND THE ORDINATION OF WOMEN

The third crucial confrontation over the logic of the nature of the Church is taking place at the present time. It has to do with the equality of women in the human community and in the Church. It began in the movement for women's suffrage earlier in this century. For the Church, and particularly for the Episcopal Church, it focuses on the issue of the opening of the ministries of presbyter and bishop to women. That the question has never seriously been faced before in the Church's history is, I believe, due to cultural and sociological assumptions—sheer *goy* assumptions. Those assumptions, as in the first and the nineteenth centuries, can still be clothed in scriptural and traditional arguments, and in arguments from divine and natural law. They are, however, *goy* assumptions, and the Bible's view of the nature of the Church makes that clear.

So did the section on Renewal in Ministry of the 1968 Lambeth Conference, which found no conclusive reasons for withholding ordination to the priesthood from women, and then went on to state:

The appeal to scripture and tradition deserves to be taken with the utmost seriousness. To disregard what we have received from the apostles, and the inheritance of Catholic Christendom, would be most inappropriate for a Church for which the authority of scripture and tradition stands high . . . It appears that the *tradition* flowing from the early Fathers and the medieval Church that a woman is incapable of receiving Holy Orders reflects biological assumptions about the nature of woman and her relation to man which are considered unacceptable in the light of modern knowledge and biblical study and have been generally discarded today. If the ancient and medieval assumptions about the social role and inferior status of women are no longer accepted, the appeal to tradition is virtually reduced to the observation that there happens to be no precedent for ordaining women to be priests. The New Testament does not encourage Christians to think that nothing should be done for the first time." (Lambeth Conference 1968, p. 106)

That, though, is basically an argument *against* the arguments against the ordination of women. My contention is that the logic of what Israel and the Church are by nature *requires* the opening of the possibility of ordination to every order within the Church to every one of its members, once the issue is raised. If that is not possible for non-Jewish Christians, then *goy* clothing, to use St. Paul's figure, is taking precedence over our being clothed in baptism in Jesus Christ. If that is not possible for Christians of races whose fitness only for slavery, by the standards of this world, came to be justified by invocation of divine Providence and natural law, then *goy* clothing is taking precedence over our being clothed in baptism in Jesus Christ. If that is not possible for a sex whose fitness only for submissiveness and childbearing, by the standards of this world, came also to be justified by invocation of divine Providence and natural law, then *goy* clothing is taking precedence over our being clothed in baptism in Jesus Christ.

Every order of ministry in the Church must be expressive of the nature of the Church as the non-*goy*, non-ethnic *ekklesia* of God. If they are not, then the Church's witness is lacking in integrity and credibility precisely because of the Church's own essential nature. Arguments that Christian priesthood is by nature masculine, or exclusively *goy* in one kind of way, are reflective of the kind of *goy*-justifying religion challenged by the God of Israel and of Jesus Christ. They are blasphemously subversive of the intrinsic nature of what Israel and the Church are by virtue of the call of God.

Therein lies the issue before the Episcopal Church. As we face it, both in terms of the Philadelphia ordinations and the 1976 General Convention, I suggest that we see it and live with it in the perspective of the Bible's view of what is essential about us as God's people.

chapter 19

THE RE-ORDERING OF
THE MINISTRY

Michael Marshall

The place of women in the Church is not simply an ecclesiastical squabble; it is a vital question of our day, and an essential part of the witness and challenge of the Christian Church to our civilization. We *must* get it right, not simply for the sake of Church order, but as part of our witness to, and care for, the world. Clearly, in our recent past we have got it very wrong indeed, and this will not make the debate any easier. No one would wish to defend the unjust and inadequate role of women in the Church in recent history. It is the purpose of this essay, however, to show that there are very considerable theological reasons for continuing the practice of the Church in ordaining only men to the office and order of a bishop in the Church of God.

CLEARING THE GROUND—WHAT IS THE QUESTION??

We are NOT talking about "women in the ministry." For far too long the Church has produced a strange species called "clergymen" and they have played the role of a "one man band"—Mr. Minister. The real injustice and distortion of the past is that this particular species, which is unscriptural and untraditional, has kept many men as well as women out of the ministry. At last—largely through the economic crisis, and also through the inspiration of the charismatic revival in the Church— we are beginning to see that all baptized men and women are "ministers." It is as though the Church should put a notice over its Noah's Ark: "No passengers aboard this ship: crew only." For Baptism was our ordination and every baptized man, woman and child is baptized to serve in the ministry of the Church. The charismatic renewal has awak-

ened many men and women to a new and deeper understanding of
their baptismal responsibilities. This is the true priesthood of all believers, because through our baptism we are made members of the Body
of Christ, and partake in his essential nature, which is that of a priest
in his relation to his Father and to the world. The Church is that priestly
body, and all its members partake of Christ's own unique and total
priesthood.

So we may ask: What is the distinctive nature of the *ordained* priesthood—more correctly called the presbyterate? "An essential element
in the ordained ministry is its responsibility for "oversight" (*episcope*). . . . Presbyters are joined with the bishop in his oversight of the
Church. . . ." *(The Canterbury Statement).* So the essential nature of the
role of the bishop/apostle is that of oversight: "Take heed to yourselves
and to all the flock, in which the Holy Spirit has made you overseers,
to feed the church of the Lord which he purchased with his own blood"
(Acts 20 verse 28). But this is not a role which excludes all other ministries: rather, it enables them and gives cohesion to them. In the early
Church this left plenty of room for the prophets and healers, and all the
other charismatic ministries—in fact, wherever the charismatic was
most in evidence there was needed the structure and order of the
sacrament in the person of the bishop or his delegate—the presbyter.

Can we rediscover the nature of that oversight and its relationship to
all the other ministries? Clearly, there was an essential interdependence in this basic model which both the priest of the Middle Ages and
the preacher-minister of the Reformation lost in their domination over
the whole body. Cranmer, in insisting on a congregation present both
at Mass and at the daily office, is hinting at a different model for the total
life of the Church. There must be this essential *interdependence* between the bishop (or the presbyter) and all the other ministers of which
the deacon is the type. So Jesus, in St. Luke's Gospel, included in his
apostolic band women who "ministered to him" and the word used is
diakoneo (St. Luke 8:3). Sadly, this interdependence has been lost: the
interdependence between the sacramental and the charismatic: between the oversight of the Church and all other ministries.

There are healthy signs that the true model of the Church could be
re-established in our day. The question before the Church, therefore,
is *not* primarily whether women should be admitted to the office of
bishop and overseer of the Church of God. The question is rather how
all baptized men and women can rediscover their ministry within the
life of the whole community, in which the Holy Spirit has set men as
overseers. Such a reordering of ministry would then clear the ground
for the secondary question: should we reverse the Judaistic-Christian
tradition of four thousand years and initiate a feminine oversight—
(*episcope*)—of the people of God?

There are three main fundamental reasons why we simply cannot and must not do this.

1: THE CLAIM OF THEOLOGY— THE METHODOLOGY OF THEOLOGY

Anglicans are committed to a particular discipline in the way they do their theology. They do not isolate the Bible from tradition and they do not set up tradition over the Bible. The Lambeth Quadrilateral—as it is sometimes called—compels the Anglicans to do their theology in a particular way. The Bible, tradition, the spirit of the age, and the place of conscience, are four reference points in this work of theology.

a. The teaching of the Bible and the mind of Christ

It is rather surprising that the early Israelites were unique in their rejection of a female priesthood in the Old Testament and stood out so strongly against the cultural conditions of the age in which the female priesthood was the norm. They had prophetesses and, indeed, women judges, and women held a strong place in the life of Judaism. Nevertheless, after some struggles, the Israelites were distinctive in rejecting the practice of all the other religions around them in maintaining only a male priestly line and in speaking of God as male. (This was not of course the only way in which they stuck out like a sore thumb against the cultural conditions of the contemporary religious climate—they were also unique in their rejection of polytheism.)

So Jesus, in the New Testament, initiated only a male apostolate. We cannot initiate any other apostolate since all priesthood is derived from him by faith and the Church must not "by works" initiate any other priesthood—indeed it cannot. One could contend that Jesus was culturally conditioned in this matter and yet it is hard to think of the Christ of the New Testament as culturally conditioned to this extent in a matter which is so at the heart of the life of the Church. Indeed, it is hard to think of him as culturally conditioned at all in essential matters of principle, for he is the one who could stand before men with stones in their hands and say: "It is written . . . but I say to you." Among his closest disciples he had many women "collaborators," and his first recorded resurrection appearance was to a woman and not to a man. Paul continues the tradition in this matter, both as a Jew and as a Christian and, while holding the Church in the house of Lydia, nevertheless sees the oversight of the Church as only male. The teaching of the Bible and the mind of Christ is that the oversight of the people of God must be male and not female: "Women did not receive the call to the apostolate of the Twelve and therefore to the ordained ministry" (Speech on April 12th, 1975, by Pope Paul).

The protagonist for women bishops, however, would contend that on this matter we cannot follow the biblical tradition because Jesus and Paul were culturally conditioned against women. This shows a total ignorance of the Greek and Roman world of the first and second centuries, with a Diana of the Ephesians and goddesses galore, in a society which in its sexual imagination was in many ways exactly like our own; moreover, behind the argument there lies a strange view of history and an even stranger view of theology.

The Christian believes that God's chosen people were rather carefully groomed to have unique and distinctive views, often in opposition to their surrounding culture. They were in this sense very strongly "culturally conditioned": this conditioning is sometimes called "revelation"! It is hard to believe that Jesus, for example, was so blinkered by the culture of his day in this profound issue of the nature of sexuality and of his own distinctive vocation as the priest, that he had to leave the Church for two thousand years to get it right.

But the question is even more urgent than this. It is a matter of how we do our theology. If, when we come into controversy with the prevailing spirit of the age, we write off the Bible as culturally conditioned and the Church as culturally blinkered in the past, what does this imply? *It implies that the Christian must conform to the contemporary culture: "Be ye conformed"!*

It would seem that, while we can speak of a biblical view of patriotism in healthy contrast to our own contemporary jaded and distorted view of patriotism, when it comes to the question of sexuality we are strangely reluctant to discover and re-assess a biblical view of sexuality and the relation of the sexes because it is different from that of the contemporary climate. While we can combat a contemporary mistaken view of economics by re-asserting a more biblical outlook on this matter without being branded a biblical fundamentalist, it would seem that in the crisis of sexuality in our contemporary culture we can only tamely assert that the age has got it right and the Bible has got it wrong.

b. The tradition of the Church and the mind of Christians
The second great cornerstone of theology is the tradition of the Church. Here again, in spite of a frequently changing cultural view, the Church has for two thousand years taught only a male oversight of the people of God. To the protagonist of female oversight this counts for nothing. Here again, the Church has been blinkered and culturally conditioned by the blindness and darkness of the past in matters of sexuality, awaiting the awakening and enlightening of the 20th century where, apparently, all the evidence would show that for the first time there is now a happy understanding of sexuality and a more wonderful

relation between the sexes than before. At last we have emerged from a male dominated society to an enlightenment which is free from the oppression of the Church in this matter so that men and women can be regarded as the same and interchangeable in every respect (except of course in the process of childbirth). This outlook is as untrue to history as it is ignorant of history. It is hard to think that in Dante or the society of Chaucer's *Canterbury Tales,* in Elizabethan England or in the time of St. Teresa of Avila there was a male chauvinist domination! However, a total ignorance of history is the best qualification to rewrite it and we are encouraged in this argument to write off two thousand years of Christian tradition in this matter because it belongs to the unenlightened ignorance of the Church, blinkered by surrounding culture and a false obedience to its foundation and its founder.

A wrong parallel is sometimes drawn here with the rejection of slavery or the admission of Gentiles to the Church. However, in the case of the former, the protagonists fail to point out that it was precisely because Christians refused to follow the cultural conditioning of the day that they were opposed to a particular and distorted form of commercial slavery. In the case of the latter, ignorant alike of Romans 15 and Acts 11, they fail to realize the process by which the Church arrived at its decision to open its gates to Gentiles. It was precisely because they looked back *to their traditions* and found substantial quotations and theological insights from the prophets of the past, that they felt able (against their own cultural prejudices) to admit Gentiles to the Church. It was their tradition which gave them that uncomfortable dialogue with their own contemporary prejudices. So, in Acts 15, we see the Church doing its theology by taking tradition and the Bible seriously.

So the question is an important one: how do you do your theology if you write off the Bible and tradition when they stand in contrast to the prevailing spirit of the age?

c. The counsel of the Churches

It is sometimes maintained that the ecumenical argument (against proceeding simply as the Church of England without waiting for other Christian Churches to make up their minds) is only an argument based upon expediency and should at best only delay action on this matter. But here again it is a strange view of the work of theology. Where have all the ecumenists gone? On this vital issue we are in danger of turning our backs on years of ecumenical growth and trust. That would be bad enough, for it will undoubtedly sever us for the foreseeable future from any communion with the Roman Catholic Church of the West or the Orthodox Church of the East—five-eighths of the whole Christian world. But there is a theological consideration at the heart of this.

Apparently the protagonists are happy to do their theology, having written off not only the Bible and the tradition of the Church, but two-thirds of their fellow Christians in the process. At this moment in history above all others, we proceed with an isolationist's view of the Church in this, the most important theological debate of the day. In other words, the counsel of the Church is ignored and again the question is: how do we do our theology? The reply is clear: on all thorny issues we follow the spirit of the age and the motivation of our own conscience. It must be said, however, that this is a new way of doing theology—no, more than that, it is not Christian theology in any recognizable form and we should realize that this is so.

2: THE PLACE OF SYMBOL IN CHRISTIAN SPIRITUALITY

For those who are familiar with the medieval debate concerning nominalism and realism, it is not necessary to say very much more than to point out that this same debate is still with us in a different key. The debate of the Middle Ages concerned the Corpus Christi in its sacramental form—the Eucharist. The debate today is centered around the nature of the *mystical* Corpus Christi—the Church, the people of God. It must be even more powerfully expressed. The study of the Church is not simply the study of an organization. It is a sacrament and its form expresses that total reconciliation which is the good news of the Gospel: the reconciliation of flesh and spirit, of heaven and earth. For the Christian, the body and the form are a sacrament: an outward and visible *sign* of an inward reality. If we sever the relationship between outward form and inward reality, or if we interchange symbols as though they did not matter, we enter into a schizoid existence and create insanity in the very deepest recesses of our experience.

We live in a world, of course, which *has* separated outward form from interior meaning. That is part of the sickness and sadness of our schizoid world. We live in a world in which the outward and visible form gives no clue to the interior meaning, and that is part of the bewilderment and pain of living in our society. So, in any study of sexuality, the Christian is committed to exploring that relationship between opposites and seeking a complementary union because of the physical difference signified by the outward and visible form of the difference between a man and a woman. To put it bluntly: men and women are *not* the same things with different fittings! The different fittings indicate an interior difference at the level of the spirit. It would be fatal to be too certain that we can readily and easily define, through a study of recent history and the victorian outlook, the precise nature of that difference. That is not the substance of the argument. Rather the very nature of sacramental theology compels us to explore the difference between the sexes and their mutual interdependence by starting in the realm of the physical.

"Love cannot and must not dispense with matter, any more than can the soul . . . Just as Spirit is never so enfranchised from matter as to be able to reject it, so every union of love must begin on the material basis of sensible confrontation and knowledge. It is a fundamental law of creative union that the fusion of spiritual apexes presupposes a coincidence of their bases." *The Eternal Feminine,* by Henri de Lubac, S.J.

If our discussion is not rooted in this kind of sacramental symbolism it fails to be rooted at all. We live in an age of the new gnostic who deliberately wishes to bypass the image and the symbol, the earth and the flesh, the body and material. Little wonder, since we have made such a mess of these. But the Christian is committed not to bypassing them but to transcending them, and taking them to where they belong, so that in the end there will be "neither Jew nor Greek, bond nor free, male nor female." But that does not point to a future which has bypassed the differences between cultures and nations, classes and sexes, living in a dull and grey asexual society. All these have to be picked up and taken to a richer and fuller dimension, where sexuality will mean more, not less. Of course we know that contemplation moves beyond images, but it does not bypass them so much as surpass them. It transcends them and picks them up to a higher reality and to a realm of greater significance, of which that much neglected feast of the Transfiguration is the type in our Lord's self-revelation. Of course, at a time like this, we are strongly tempted to bypass those very areas of our life in which we have seen so many pitfalls. We live in a materialistic age: would to God we could bypass the image, the symbol, the flesh, matter, mother, mater, and materialism. But that is not the good news of the Gospel. The Gospel consists of going on beyond what is natural and taking it into the supernatural. Paul says: "First those things that are natural, and then those things that are supernatural." Sadly, there are many gurus and disciples today who would flee the natural and the symbol and split it off from the supernatural, leaving it to fester unredeemed.

Perhaps this schizoid gnosticism is nowhere more apparent than in the alienation between head and body in every sense of that phrase. Our body politic is alienated between those who are insane because they only use their head and those who are bored because they only use their hands. "The madman is not the man who has lost his reason but the man who has lost everything except his reason" (G. K. Chesterton). The body politic is divided between head and body: our personalities are divided between head and body. The spirit of the age has brought into this alienation only a spirit of competition. In contrast, the spirit of the Gospel, in the name of reconciliation, speaks only of interdependence: "The head cannot say to the body, I have no need of you, neither can the body say to the head, I have no need of you." Whatever the difference between the sexes may be, it is through emphasizing their difference in the name of interdependence, and not through seeking their similarities in the spirit of competition, that our common life will once again be healed. This will go right across the board, and only Christianity has the model and the theology of the body politic, ecclesiastical and physical, which is sufficiently large and diverse to rescue the present unhappy and divisive debate which is at the very heart of our common life, not only in the matter of sexuality but at every level.

I cannot believe that the people of God would be the same with a matriarchal oversight (*episcope*) as with a patriarchal. These two are not interchangeable, and perhaps if we spoke a language which endowed all impersonal nouns with a gender, we would know that no language in the world speaks of "father earth"—it is "mother earth"; there is no bypassing the earth, however "spiritual" the discussion may become. The challenge is a profound one. I believe that the place of "mother" is crucial to this generation. She has become either a music hall joke or a problem as a tyrant in psychology. It is not incidental that often behind a saint in the Church there is a remarkable mother, and perhaps we shall not have any saints in this age until the place of "mother" in our society is rediscovered. The Middle Ages were perhaps in danger of placing woman above man, and above God in the strong emphasis on mariolatry. Nevertheless, the madonnas in every village church across Europe must have been an effective sign to a society, speaking as they did of a reconciliation which our age has distorted by denying women their true place in society, in the Church, and in our psychology. Both male and female have become distorted: mother earth and everything that is of "mater" is judged only in relation to a distorted male image. How right the *A Rule for a New Brother* is when it says: "Mary, the mother of the Lord, must have a place in your life." When iconoclasts tore down madonnas they did more to our consciousness than we perhaps realize. Mother is not immaterial: matter matters for the Christian. I am not here advocating anything less than a strenuous struggle to understand again something of the place of the feminine in our life and, above all, in the concept of the city. In the end it will be the new Jerusalem which is the "mother of us all" and the interdependence between male and female is the way by which our cities will be redeemed from being sick, soulless, masculine, heady centers of loneliness and alienation.

3: THE CONTEMPORARY CHALLENGE

Following from what I have said earlier, if this is really the heart of the matter—if it is not simply an ecclesiastical squabble but if the debate touches on our whole understanding of the creation and our part within it—then the debate about a feminine oversight of the Church and women bishops is a far-flung and vitally important topic. The debate has not yet really begun. Could it be that there is a relation between the present crisis about sexuality and the crisis of materialism? The Protestant work ethic which has pervaded the outlook of Western society for the past four hundred years has come to the end of the road. Tawney's thesis, *Religion and the rise of capitalism,* is all too true. If our only criterion for handling the earth and our environment is a masculine one which, in the name of productivity, invites competition, then little wonder that our environment is in the sad and weary condition that it is.

The feminine must tame this masculine domination which shows in every aspect of our common life. It will tame it, not by competing with it; it will tame it, not by copying it; it will tame it, not by being interchangeable with it. It will tame it only by that union at the heart of which is love. For in the act of procreation, as in the dance, there cannot be superiority or inferiority; there cannot be envy or competition—only a complementary union. There will be much humor and irony, subtleties and many surprises. At some point that union will reach out for a total form which can express this ultimate reconciliation. There is a Body waiting. It is the Resurrection Body of Christ of which we are members, and in the end that Body will be the new creation, in which, on the other side of differentiation, there is that true and full reconciliation in which there is "neither Greek nor Jew, bond nor free, male nor female."

SUMMARY

The Church must not simply follow the cultural conditioning of this age in this sector of Western society and in this little island. It must rather seek to communicate with the spirit of the age, to confront it and challenge it both by yea and by nay. In the common life of the Body of Christ on earth there must be a sacramental sign of the interdependence of the sexes; between the head and the body; between oversight and ministry. Neither can dispense with the other. Both are interdependent. The shape and model of the Church needs this reorientation. The liturgy of the Church will be a demonstration of this interdependence between *episcope* and deaconing: a dialogue and a dance.

We may have to go back into our tradition like "wise scribes," bringing out both the old as well as the new, if we are to discover the rich diversity of the world of Chaucer or the humor of the Shakespearean comedies which so often are based on the exchange of role, but never on its identity. There have been chapters in the history of our Western culture when women were not hindered; it is hard to see St. Hilda or St. Theresa as oppressed by male chauvinism!

All this will be part of our debate as we seek to recover such a harmony at the heart of the life of the Church. Such a discussion might bring us to a better understanding both of the nature of the episcopate of the Church, and also the nature of sexuality. There have been few periods in history less able to make a far reaching decision which springs from a deep understanding of ministry and the nature of sexuality. The real debate has scarcely begun, and ought not to be foreclosed by an arbitrary schismatic decision by one minute section of the Church.

chapter 20

THE PRIEST AS ENCHANTER

Urban T. Holmes

There is no issue in Christian thought today—particularly the doctrine of the priesthood—which can avoid the critical focus of contemporary theology: the doctrine of revelation. The question is how does the transcendent God make himself known in a way that is capable of being perceived, interpreted, and acted upon in history *at this present time.*[1]

In some circles revelation is thought of as a message given in ancient times which now only needs to be believed and obeyed. This view of revelation involves those who hold it in an immense task of translating ancient meanings into modern meanings. It also makes assumptions about the relation between Creator and creature which raises two serious theological problems.[2] First, it implies that there is a difference between God's *presence* and God's act of self-revelation. For if revelation is only a message received in the past, it means either that God is not present today, or that he is present only in silence. Second, if revelation ended a long time ago, then there is a special kind of history which is revelatory and no longer present, and there is present history which is not revelatory. Christians who hold this view almost inevitably take a negative attitude toward their own times. It is very difficult for them to avoid lapsing into that nostalgia for the "golden age" which Bonhoeffer rightly called "the leap of death."

I believe that God is present now and that this presence is inevitably an act of self-revelation in our ordinary history. The spiritual hunger which many of us see in the Church today, exemplified in the revival of the retreat movement, the new interest in meditation, the explosion of personal witness, and the rise of prayer groups—as well as a renewed sense of the Holy Spirit among us—is expressive of the desire to experience God-making-himself-known-to-man-now. This cannot be rendered intelligible unless we believe God reveals himself at the present in the ordinary lives of contemporary persons.

Furthermore, revelation is the experience of God in relationship; it is intersubjectivity. Gabriel Moran, a Roman Catholic lay brother, has said: "Revelation is . . . what communities experience."[3] Revelation is the sense of being called into being within a saving social reality by that which *transcends* that social phenomenon but which makes itself known *in* our present history in the context of a significant interaction with others. Since all of history is in God, man may encounter the revelatory invitation in any dimension of his life.

If we ask what this has to do with the priest, the answer is: "Everything." What was described in the previous paragraph was the priestly community. A working definition of a priest is one who leads in awakening persons to the revelatory character of their community experience in their present history. If this is true, then obviously the nature of the priesthood as far as the Christian faith and the Church Catholic is concerned cannot be understood apart from the doctrine of revelation. Therefore, the problem of what it means to be a priest is integral to the critical focus of contemporary theology.

The priestly vocation is not always considered within this setting today. Ministerial studies abound and the art of pastoral care has a rapidly expanding bibliography. We have tended to set these studies within a psychological and sociological framework. As far as it goes, this can be very beneficial.

But sociology has tended to describe priesthood as a role function within an institution. It would be unfair to imply that this has been the only interpretation offered in the name of sociology, but Seward Salisbury is representative of that discipline when he writes: "The clerical task is a profession, a career, and an occupation."[4] By "profession" he means the rendering of service, by "career" he describes the doing of this service over a lifetime, and by "occupation" he refers to the fact that it is done as gainful employment.

The sociological theory that lies behind this is that the dominant function of religion, which the priest represents, is to adjust, adapt, and integrate the social structures within which it operates, to promote their stability, and to serve the well-being of their members as good citizens by the legitimation and reinforcement of the society's values. The great French sociologist, Emile Durkheim, argued that society exudes a certain effervescence, which can be experienced as "religious" and leads to the attribution of transcendence to what is, in fact, society itself. In this way, while seeming to serve God the religious specialist is actually serving the society and its members. The true existence of Being, which transcends the social world and yet is concerned for and acts in the social world, is not necessary in such an understanding of religion and is frequently ignored or even denied as the source of the adjustment, adaptation, and integration of society.

Aside from the fact that this can easily infer that Karl Marx was right and religion does maintain the *status quo* and not the revolutionary needs of the oppressed—an image of the priesthood which finds considerable Old Testament support—it has also promoted the idea that to be a priest is principally to serve the prevailing society in ministering to its members in accordance with that society's expectations. This notion has some roots in the Constantinian Church, where the priest was responsible for the education of the society's citizens, for the social welfare distributed to the society's poor and infirm, and for the communication of governmental decrees. It was symbolized in the priest's civil function as registrar of births, marriages, and deaths—a task now performed by the clerk of court. It has a degree of contemporary expression in the advocacy over the last fifty years of the *professional* model of the priesthood.

The model of the professional, which Salisbury described as one of service, may be further considered as the work of one who has mastered certain skills based upon a theoretical body of knowledge in which he is certified and for which the members of society recognize their need. The need for the ability to predict and control, as valued in a technological culture such as ours, dominates this model. I think there is good in the professional model, as far as it goes, but there is a fundamental theological flaw within it as well. This flaw—like the theory that religion exists to adjust, adapt, and integrate the society by the legitimation and reinforcement of its values—is that *there is no need in this model of the priest for the actuality of transcendent being.*

I know a bishop who instructs parish search committees that one question they must ask of prospective candidates is: "Do you believe in God?" I talked with the chairman of such a search committee, who acknowledged her initial amazement at this suggestion of the bishop. She told me: "At first we thought this was very strange, but we asked it as he suggested. While no one said, 'No,' some of the 'Yes' answers sounded very much like 'No.' " She added, not just as an afterthought, "How can they be priests?"

The problem is compounded by a further fact. If we define the priesthood as a role within a social structure or institution (the Church) that is part of society, then the possibilities for that role are the possibilities that lie within the society. We live in a secular society, for which the category of revelation is foreign, even repugnant. I am speaking of our behavior, not what we profess. As Harvey Cox has said, secularization is the fact of living in a closed society, secularism is the believe that this is in effect all there is.[5] It is enough for my purpose to point out that secularization has the effect of imposing only a secular expectation on any role function within it, including the priesthood.

Some years ago, one of my students came to me in great distress. He was doing field work at a boys' training school in Wisconsin and one of the case workers had met him with the challenge: "What are you doing here that is any different from what I am doing?" His distress was born not just of the fact that there was no language with which he could make this *savant* of the secular society understand his own self-perception, but much more that he, the child of a secular culture, could not find the words to make clear to himself—much less anyone else—the call to serve our risen Lord.

Max Weber, the great German sociologist and contemporary of Durkheim, characterized what I am describing by saying that we live today in a "disenchanted world."[6] What this colorful phrase means is that we live today with no *socialized* expectation of the evidence of God's presence in the world. It is not a part of our collective representation. Society does not tell us that the whole world is alive with proof of transcendent glory. If any one testified to having seen "little people" or having been visited in a dream by an "angel" or having heard a heavenly call, our first thought would be of hospitalization.

No one believes in God now as he would have two hundred years ago. If we believe, it is not because we have a common consensus within society that interacts with the Church to reinforce and refine that belief. We believe in the absence of any positive socialization, if not in the face of considerable negative influence. Our language, for example, no longer emerges from and undergirds a sense of the transcendent presence. The word "monster," to illustrate the point, comes originally from the Latin *monstrare,* meaning "to show," and is derived from medieval man's belief that any physical aberration in human or subhuman animal life was the direct result of divine intervention for purposes known only to God. This never occurs to us who understand genetic accidents. The word "enthusiasm," to cite another example, means now only to be excited about something with accompanying phenomena readily explained by psychological "triggers" and the flow of the ductless glands. The word comes, however, from a Greek root meaning to have "God within you," denoting that to which man once commonly attributed the experience.

The effect of our disenchanted society is to rob the priest of any normal, common-sense, or socialized expectation as *one who mediates the presence of a transcendent reality.* This is to deprive him of any structural definition of his role as that person who awakens mankind to the revelatory character of their community experience. It strongly influences us to think of the priest in terms of a socially constructed reality—to cite Berger and Luckmann's term—that discounts any human resources that lie below the sociocultural definition of man and that ignores any possibility of a transcendent vocation for you and me.

Priesthood in any such narrowing of definition becomes meaningless, because it is of the very character of priesthood to be rooted in the living possibility of revelation effected by the personal relationship of man to God present in his ordinary existence. A way of putting this is to say that *the priest is an enchanter.*

Some years ago, when about to undergo surgery, I had the following fantasy. I was being wheeled down the hall to surgery on one of those carts with which most of us are familiar and I thought to myself: What if I looked up at the surgeon (who was a friend of mine) and said, "Dick, do you know what you're doing?" What if he had replied, "No, but I have an eschatological hope!" Dick is a devout Roman Catholic, but in spite of that, I know what I would have done in the face of such an answer. The irony is that the answer *is* appropriate for the priest. There is a difference. Dick is a professional surgeon, who must be in control. The business of the priest is to awaken us to that which cannot be controlled: God's self-revelation in our community experience.

It seems to me that we must come to grips with that difference and recover the vocation of the priest to enable persons to perceive the revealing presence of God in their ordinary lives by refusing to let the priestly calling be defined purely in structural terms. There is no problem in speaking of the priest *at least* as a professional, but the categories of the professional are peripheral to the core of the definition of a priest.

Barbara Myerhoff, an anthropologist, described in her recent book, *The Peyote Hunt,* a religious specialist among the Huichol Indians of Mexico who combines in one person the classical sociological definition of the priest and the eccentricity of the shaman. The institutional role, with all its predictable expectations, is joined to a person who possesses a certain personal integrity as he lives on the margins of the social structures.[7] He is both a controlled professional, if you will, and an unpredictable agent of surprise. This is a concrete representation of the model I have in mind for the contemporary Christian priest, who is both professional and enchanter.

Such a model catches up Margaret Mead's argument that religious communities need to be both conservative and innovative. The day has passed, I trust, when we glibly offer the false polarities between the mystic and the prophet or the traditionalist and the pioneer. Martin Luther King, to name one prominent Christian witness, embodied all these things. There needs to be a constant dialogue within every priest, wherein he settles for no one position. It is a vocation that both must be open to conserve and to innovate and must be capable of reduction to no single category or stereotype.

The need then is to rescue the central notion of priesthood from the categories of control, such as are necessary in concepts of information retrieval, mastery of skills, job descriptions, and evaluative measurement. We need to recover for the priest the mediating function by expecting not that he be something different from this, but that he be something *more* than this. He should be acquainted with realms of human experience that exist in the twilight of our learning, in the depth of human existence, and in the possibilities of God's future. The priest needs to affirm the liminal quality of the shaman, even if the model of the shaman *per se* is not always helpful.

This notion is very difficult to realize in a technological society, which is most uncomfortable with the unpredictable. It is even troublesome to find images to express in an operational manner the priest as enchanter: one who leads us into the depths of human experience that underlie the structures of a society committed to planning rather than hoping.[8] Myerhoff, in her most helpful discussion of the religious specialist among the Huichol, offers the concept of the priest as the leader of pilgrimage, that movement away from the routinized center of our existence to the center of life's meaning found "out there." This suggests that the ground of being is more often than not discerned when we consciously strip ourselves of the trappings of role and status that make up most of our daily life—just as our Lord was lead outside the city walls to be stripped and to die.

Most of us are familiar with the image of the pilgrimage as a journey to a distant place, if for no other reason than we have read Chaucer's *Canterbury Tales.* Few of us, I daresay, have consciously gone on such a pilgrimage. There is, however, another kind of pilgrimage, which perhaps touches closer to our own lives and can illuminate the meaning of enchantment: the inner journey. Robert Ornstein, a psychologist, points out that each of us has two brains: the left hemisphere, which controls the right side, and the right hemisphere, which guides the left side. The left brain deals in a world of prediction, analysis, and logic. The right brain lives in a world of spontaneity, surprise, and free association. Pilgrimage as an inner journey, can be seen as a *movement* back and forth between the two domains of our two brains.

The value of Ornstein's paradigm is that it possesses a scientific aura, perhaps even credentials. Our society, obsessed with science, has lived too long in half a brain, which is the reason we understand our world as disenchanted. The goal is to live in both sides, and the question is how the priest as leader of the pilgrimage can help to achieve this or, to put it another way, can evoke once again in our experience the sense of enchantment that awakens us to the revelation in ordinary living. This is in a sense impossible, because we are speaking of a mystic art. No one can reduce the methods of Picasso, T. S. Eliot, or Ingmar Bergman to computer tapes, and it would be a contradiction to attempt a job description of the enchanter. We can only point to certain qualities that some observe in the enchanter and his priestly arts.

I would include in such a description, first, a singleness of mind—Jesus called it purity of heart—coupled with an inner silence and a reverent iconoclasm. The priest who would be an instrument of enchantment must flirt with being boring, absentminded, and heretical. Just as there is a thin line between genius and psychosis, so is there between purity of heart and banality. The pompous dogmatist and the "bull in the china shop" are both acting out of fear. A reverent iconoclasm and an inner silence operate out of hope.

Secondly, there is in the enchanter a visible, happy incongruity born of his recognition that in God there is the coincidence of opposites joined with an awareness that he himself is not God. The "opposites" lie in the priest as still unreconciled contradictions. By way of illustration: On a flight from Chicago to Nashville I was seated next to a man who informed me that he did not "buy" religion. Over Indianapolis one of the plane's engines caught fire and we had to make an emergency landing. As soon as we were safely down, I muttered, "Thank God! Now I hope they break out the booze!" My fellow passenger, equally relieved that we were safe, asked if I had been praying. "Of course," I said. "What else?" He went on, as if he had trapped me in some inconsistency, "I don't understand how you can pray and ask for a drink in almost the same breath." For once I thought of a good comeback on the spot instead of the next day. "If you understood that," I told him, "then you'd 'buy' religion!"

In the third place, the effective priest combines within himself the toughness of the seasoned pastor with the transparency of the child. This is uncontrived. I think we all know when someone is playing at being this way. He used to be a caricature of Bing Crosby in *Going My Way*. Now it is more likely to come across as an imitation of the "waterfront priest," affecting a kind of "mod" look with a holy gleam in the eye.

Fourth, I have never met an enchanter who did not possess a certain wholesome earthiness. The Judaeo-Christian tradition has been its own worst enemy to the degree that it has incorporated into its own life that peculiar brand of Middle Eastern asceticism, characterized by an obsessive fear of the material world, which has been reinforced by centuries of recurring Puritanism. Its Christ is docetic, its sacraments are banal, and its sense of the holy is sanitized. The effective priest is not a dilettante or a "shrinking violet." The idea that "cleanliness is next to godliness" originated with the rabbis of the Talmud, reflecting their anxiety over pollution. It strikes me as quite inconsistent with the Incarnation. The priest who would awaken us to God's self-revelation cannot so easily avoid the "darker rooms" inhabited by the tellurian spirits and the chothonic powers of the world.

Finally, the enchanter is one whose strength is his weakness-made-manifest. He takes St. Paul's injunction seriously that in our weakness is our strength (2 Corinthians 12:10). In the foolishness of man God becomes for us a living reality. The priest is the jester, the court fool, who abrogates the aggressive seriousness of the "successful" for the incongruity of victory in the midst of failure.

Much more could be said, but it is important that we understand that these and any other descriptions of the person of the priest-enchanter are not character traits to be learned, but are by-products of a quality of life. That quality of life arises from the cultivation of those areas of our existence that resist social definition in role and status and are not reducible to any cultural ideology.

I recall many years ago being challenged by an up-and-coming naval officer, who had had just enough to drink to overcome a certain conditioned reticence in the presence of the clergy. For some time he pressed me with personal questions, and finally explained his actions by saying, "I must know what makes you priests 'tick'." I have always been grateful to this example of America's finest; but after trying to figure out the answer for years, I have decided there is no answer if a priest is what God calls him to be. The enchanter is a man of the twilight, that characteristic coloring of known-and-yet-unknown, where the mystery of God and the longing of the human spirit meet in the light of revelation.

NOTES

1. Wolfhart Pannenberg, *Jesus: God and Man,* trans., Lewis L. Wilkins and Duane A. Priebe (Philadelphia: Westminster Press, 1968), p. 131; "The problem of revelation has become the fundamental question in modern theology." Cf. Gabriel Moran, *The Present Revelation: The Search for Religious Foundations* (New York: Herder and Herder, 1972), p. 22.

2. I am indebted to Dietrich Ritschel, *Memory and Hope* (New York: Macmillan Company, 1967), pp. 17–18, for making these problems so clear.

3. Gabriel Moran, op. cit., p. 228.

4. Seward Salisbury, *Religion in American Culture: A Sociological Interpretation* (Homewood, Ill.: Dorsey Press, 1964), p. 206.

5. Harvey Cox, *The Secular City: Secularization and Urbanization in Theo-*

logical Perspective (New York: Macmillan Company, 1965), pp. 20–21.

6. A concise summary of this key concept in Max Weber in relation to other nineteenth-century thought of the same kind can be found in George Lichtheim, "Alienation," *International Encyclopedia of the Social Sciences*, vol. 1 (New York: Crowell Collier and Macmillian, 1968), pp. 264–268.

7. Barbara Myerhoff, *The Peyote Hunt* (Ithaca: Cornell University Press, 1974), pp. 94–101.

8. The distinction between "planning" and "hoping" is worked out in an essay by Jürgen Moltmann, *Hope and Planning*, trans. Margaret Clarkson (New York: Harper and Row, 1971), pp. 178–199. To plan is to have an anticipatory disposition to the future. To hope is to look toward that future which another, perhaps God, places at my disposal.

contributors

C. FitzSimons Allison is Rector of Grace Episcopal Church, New York, and was previously a professor of ecclesiastical history at the Virginia Theological Seminary. Dr. Allison is widely known as an author and lecturer and as a distinguished scholar of 17th-century Anglican theology.

Frederick H. Borsch is Dean of the Church Divinity School of the Pacific and was previously professor of New Testament at General Theological Seminary and Seabury-Western Seminary. He has published extensively in his field of special research, the New Testament.

Myles Bourke is Pastor of Corpus Christi Roman Catholic Church, New York, and adjunct professor of New Testament at Fordham University. He has been president of the Catholic Biblical Association.

Louis Bouyer, priest of the Oratory, is a theologian of liturgy and spirituality. He has lectured at the Institut Catholique in Paris and has published widely in the field of liturgy and spirituality.

Michael J. Buckley is a Jesuit priest and an associate professor of systematic theology at the Jesuit School of Theology at Berkeley University.

John M. Gessell is professor of Christian Ethics at the School of Theology at the University of the South, Sewanee, Tennessee. Dr. Gessell has worked in the area of liberation theology and in curriculum design in theological education.

William B. Green is professor of theology at the Episcopal Seminary of the Southwest, Austin, Texas, and a former chaplain at Vassar College.

Harvey H. Guthrie, Jr. is an Old Testament scholar and is presently the Dean of the Episcopal Divinity School in Cambridge, Massachusetts.

183

Urban T. Holmes is the Dean of the School of Theology at the University of the South. His field of special interest is theology and culture, and he is the author of a number of books and articles in that field.

Thomas Hopko is a priest of the Orthodox Church in America and a member of the faculty of St. Vladimir's Orthodox Theological Seminary.

Joseph Kitagawa is Dean of the Divinity School of the University of Chicago. His published work in the history of religions has also served to increase interest in that field.

John Macquarrie is a Canon of Christ Church and Lady Margaret Professor of Divinity, Oxford University. He was formerly a professor at Union Seminary in New York.

Michael Marshall was a well-known preacher at All Saints, Margaret Street in London before his selection as Bishop of Woolwich. He has lectured widely in the United States and is well known as a radio preacher.

Quentin Quesnell is a Roman Catholic New Testament scholar and the author of a number of books in this field. He has served as chairman of the Department of Theology at Marquette University, Milwaukee, and is presently doing research on theological methodology.

Herbert J. Ryan, S.J., is associate professor of historical theology at Loyola University at Los Angeles. He has taught at the General Theological Seminary in New York and has a wide range of experience in ecumenical contact, both formal and informal, between the Roman Catholic Church and the Anglican Communion.

Massey H. Shepherd, Jr., is professor of liturgics and Vice-Dean of the Church Divinity School of the Pacific. He is author of numerous works in the area of early church history and liturgical studies.

Robert E. Terwilliger is the Suffragan Bishop of Dallas. He was the founder and director of Trinity Institute, New York, a national theological center for Episcopal clergy.

Frederica Thompsett is assistant professor of church history at Seabury-Western Theological Seminary, Evanston, Illinois. Her area of special interest and research is the English Reformation Church.

Arthur A. Vogel is Bishop of the Diocese of West Missouri, and prior to that was professor of systematic theology at Nashotah House. He is the author of a number of works in theology, and is a representative of the Anglican Communion to the International Anglican-Roman Catholic Consultation.

Louis Weil is professor of liturgics at Nashotah House and has previously served on the faculty of the Seminario Episcopal del Caribe. He is the author of numerous articles in the field of liturgical studies.

bibliography

Barth, Karl, *The Word of God and the Word of Man* (Boston: Pilgrim Press, 1928). Sermons on the Word of God, with an especially important treatment of the situation on Sunday morning when the preacher must proclaim the Word under God.

Botte, B., et al., *The Sacrament of Orders* (Collegeville, Minnesota: Liturgical Press, 1955). A series of scholarly essays by Roman Catholic historians, liturgical scholars, and theologians on ordination, its history and meaning.

Brown, Raymond, *Priest and Bishop, Biblical Reflections* (Paramus, N.J.: Paulist Press, 1970). A consideration of the New Testament evidence, a radical reinterpretation of traditional Roman Catholic positions.

Carey, Kenneth M., ed., *The Historic Episcopate in the Fullness of the Church* (London: Dacre Press, 1954). A response to *The Apostolic Ministry* by Anglican writers who view episcopacy as of the *bene esse* rather than the *esse* of the Church.

Chrysostom, John, *The Priesthood*, trans. W. A. Jurgens (New York: Macmillan, 1955). The discussion of priesthood by the great "silver-tongued" preacher and Father of the Eastern Church.

Dunstan, G. B., *The Sacred Ministry* (London: S.P.C.K., 1970). An ecumenical symposium on the ministry by English churchmen, chiefly Anglican.

Feuillet, Andre, *The Priesthood of Christ and His Ministers*, trans. Matthew J. O'Connell (New York: Doubleday, 1975). A study of the priesthood of Christ and its continuation in a distinct ministry in the Church based on the "high priestly prayer" of Christ in the Fourth Gospel and its ground in the Old and New Testaments. The author is Professor of Theology at the Institut Catholique in France.

187

Farmer, H. H., *The Servant of the Word* (New York: Scribner's Sons, 1942). The Christian minister as a preacher, an exposition of the uniqueness of the calling and its power.

Gore, Charles, *The Church and the Ministry* (London: Longmans Green, 1900). A classic statement of the origin and purpose of the Christian ministry from a bishop and leader of the Catholic movement in the Church of England.

Hebert, A. G., *Apostle and Bishop, A Study of the Gospel, The Ministry and the Church Community* (New York: The Seabury Press, 1963). The meaning of episcopacy as seen by an Anglican monk and biblical scholar, who was one of the earlier leaders of the Liturgical Movement in his Church.

Hewitt, Emily C. and Suzanne R. Hiatt, *Women Priests: Yes or No* (New York: The Seabury Press, 1973). This is a concise summary of the arguments for and against the ordination of women by two authors committed, both personally and theologically, to the ordination of women to the priesthood and episcopacy. It is a solid summary of the evidence seen through the authors' own filters.

Holmes, Urban T., *The Future Shape of Ministry* (New York: The Seabury Press, 1972). This is a widely used text in Episcopal seminaries, reviewing the historical development of ministry in general and priesthood in particular. It also seeks to analyze the present ministerial roles and offer some suggestions as to how we might move in the future.

Hooker, Richard, *Laws of Ecclesiastical Polity,* Book Five, (New York: E.P.Dutton, 1954). The classic exposition of the Anglican understanding of ministry and ordination, Sections LXXVII-LXXXI.

Hughes, John Jay, *Absolutely Null and Utterly Void, The Papal Condemnation of Anglican Orders, 1896* (Washington: Corpus Books, 1968). A reconsideration of the question by a Roman Catholic priest and former Anglican.

Kirk, Kenneth, ed., *The Apostolic Ministry, Essays on the History and Doctrine of the Episcopacy* (London: Hodder and Staughton, 1962). An important symposium on the origins and theology of Episcopal ministry by a group of Catholic minded scholars in the Church of England. The later editions contain a preface by Austin Farrer, reacting to the discussion the book provided.

Küng, Hans, *Why Priests: A Proposal for New Church Ministry*, trans. Robert C. Collins (New York: Doubleday, 1972). An analysis and criticism of the concept of priesthood by a liberal Roman Catholic theologian bringing the concept of priesthood itself into question.

Küng, Hans, *Apostolic Succession, Rethinking a Barrier to Unity*, Concilium, vol. 34 (Paramus, N.J.: Paulist Press, 1968). Essays on the vexed question of "valid" ordinations and the meaning of the succession from a liberal Roman Catholic point of view.

Lewis, C.S., *God in the Dock, Essays on Theology and Ethics* (Grand Rapids: Eerdmans, 1970). Chapter XI, "Priestesses in the Church?" A criticism of the proposal to ordain women to the sacramental priesthood from the standpoint of its effects on the Christian doctrine of God and the nature of the Church.

Meyer, Charles R., *Man of God: A Study of the Priesthood* (New York: Doubleday, 1974). The principal thesis of this Roman Catholic seminary professor is that the role of the priest is to lead those to whom he ministers into the experience of the mystery of God.

Ministry and Ordination: A Statement of the Doctrine of the Ministry Agreed By the Anglican Roman Catholic International Commission (New York: Morehouse-Barlow, 1973).

Moberly, R. C., *Ministerial Priesthood* (London: John Murray, 1889). A classic Anglican presentation of priesthood, its biblical origins, historical development, and theological meaning from a position both evangelical and catholic. A section deals with the question of the official Roman Catholic condemnation of the validity of Anglican ordinations.

Modern Ecumenical Documents on the Ministry (London: S.P.C.K. and New York: Morehouse-Barlow, 1975). This is a companion volume to the 1973 publication, *Modern Eucharist Agreement*. A number of disparate groups—Anglican-Roman Catholic, Lutheran-Roman Catholic, Group of Le Dombes (Reformed-Roman Catholic), and the Commission on Faith and Order of the World Council—have come to some surprisingly convergent conclusions on the nature and significance of the ministry.

Nouwen, Henri J. M., *Creative Ministry* (New York: Doubleday, 1971). The basic thesis of this book is that ministry cannot be reduced to a professional model after the manner of doctors, lawyers, engineers, etc. Ministry involves a kind of interpersonal relationship between a priest and people, which enables them to grow into their true being.

Nouwen, Henri J. M., *The Wounded Healer: Ministry in Contemporary Society* (New York: Doubleday, 1972). This book continues the theme of *Creative Ministry*, and develops an understanding of the role of the priest in which the person's own humanness becomes an effective instrument in the meditation of God's presence to people. He speaks of the Christian leader as a contemplative critic, an artist, and one who helps people from suffering for the wrong reasons.

Pellegrino, Michele, *The True Priest* (New York: Philosophical Library, 1968). A collection of writings of St. Augustine on the priesthood.

Price, Charles P., *The Ordination of Women in Theological Perspective* (Cincinnati: Forward Movement, 1974). A statement of the case for the ordination of women.

"Priests" and "Priestly Formation" in *Documents of Vatican Two* ed. by Walter Abbott (New York: Association Press, 1966). Decree on priestly training of Vatican Council Two and Life of Priests of Vatican Council Two.

Rahner, Karl, *The Identity of the Priest* (Paramus, N.J.: Paulist Press, 1969). Symposium on priesthood by liberal Roman Catholics.

Rahner, Karl, *The Priesthood*, trans. Edward Quinn (New York: Seabury Press, 1973). This series of addresses by an eminent Roman Catholic theologian consists of a mixture of theological insights and spiritual guidelines for the ministerial priesthood.

Ramsey, Michael, *The Christian Priest Today* (London: S.P.C.K., 1972). A gathering of the ordination charges on the meaning of priesthood of the former Archbishop of Canterbury given throughout his episcopate.

Ramsey, Michael, *The Gospel and the Catholic Church* (London: Longmans Green, 1956). A study of the origin and development of the form of the Church as an expression of the Gospel. The treatment of the emergence of the episcopacy is of particular significance.

Schillebeeckx, Edward, ed., *The Unifying Role of the Bishop* (New York: Concilium, 1972). A symposium on episcopacy from a liberal Catholic point of view.

Streeter, Burnett, H., *The Primitive Church, Studied with Special Reference to the Origins of the Christian Ministry* (New York: Macmillan, 1929). A study of the variety of forms of Christian ministry in the New Testament from a perspective of liberal evangelical Anglicanism.

Sykes, Norman, *Old Priest and New Presbyters* (Cambridge: Cambridge University Press, 1956). Lectures on Episcopal and Presbyterian ministries in England and Scotland since the Reformation.

Terwilliger, Robert E., *The Ordination of Men in Theological Perspective* (Cincinnati: Forward Movement, 1974). A statement of the case for a purely male priesthood.

Torrance, T. F., *Royal Priesthood*, Scottish Journal of Theology Occasional Paper, no. 3 (Edinburgh: Oliver Bord, 1955). An important exposition of the meaning of the priesthood of Christ in the epistle to the Hebrews by a Scottish Presbyterian theologian and New Testament scholar.

Von Balthazar, Hans Urs, "The Priest I want," *Elucidations* (London: Darton, Longman, and Todd, 1975). A comment on and criticism of the practice of priesthood in the post-Conciliar Church by an eminent Swiss Roman Catholic theologian and writer on spirituality.